STUDENT TEXT

CATULLUS

FOR THE AP*:
A SUPPLEMENT

HENRY V. BENDER, PH.D. &
PHYLLIS FORSYTH, PH.D.

Bolchazy-Carducci Publishers, Inc.
Wauconda, Illinois USA

*AP is a registered trademark of the College Entrance Examination Board, which was not involved in the production of, and does not endorse, this product.

General Editor:
LeaAnn A. Osburn

Cover Design & Typography:
Adam Phillip Velez

Cover Illustration:
Girl with pigeons, fifth century BC
Courtesy of the Metropolitan Museum of Art, New York

Title Page Illustration:
Craig Duncan
The Hill School, PA

Catullus for the AP˙: A Supplement
Student Text

Henry V. Bender & Phyllis Young Forsyth

© 2004 Bolchazy-Carducci Publishers, Inc.
All rights reserved

Bolchazy-Carducci Publishers, Inc.
1000 Brown Street, Unit 101
Wauconda, Illinois 60084
www.bolchazy.com

Printed in the United States of America
2004
by United Graphics

ISBN 0-86516-575-0

Library of Congress Cataloging-in-Publication Data
Catullus, Gaius Valerius.
 [Selections. 2004]
 Catullus for the AP : a supplement : student text / [edited by] Henry V. Bender & Phyllis Forsyth.
  p. cm.
 This volume is a supplement to: Catullus. Advanced placement ed. 1997. Contains the poems that are new to the 2004-05 Catullus advanced placement syllabus.
 Includes bibliographical references.
 ISBN 0-86516-575-0 (pbk : alk. paper)
 1. Latin language--Readers. 2. Love poetry, Latin. 3. Epigrams, Latin. 4. Rome--Poetry. I. Bender, Henry V., 1945- II. Forsyth, Phyllis Young. III. Title.

PA6274.A25 2004
874'.01--dc22

2004008540

Contents

Preface

Since the publication of our first Catullus text in 1998, over 15,000 copies have been used. The numerous constructive comments we have received from the many teachers and students, who continue to choose our book for their threshold study of Catullus, have informed our construction of the present volume.

Beginning in the academic year 2004-2005, the Catullus Advanced Placement Syllabus has been significantly altered. Students are now required to read almost one half of Poem 64, as well as other much shorter poems, which expose a side of the poet only hinted at by the old syllabus. To address the need for a text which places these new selections readily into the hands of students, we have constructed this special supplement.

For information on figures of speech and meters, we refer you to our first book. In the present volume, to respond to suggestions from teachers, we have added a section in which only the Latin of the poems appears. This section provides the teacher and student with a recitation opportunity by which, after study of the poems with facing vocabulary, they may each be read in class without the presence of vocabulary prompts. The presence of such a text also provides easier opportunities for oral or written assessments of a student's real mastery of the material.

All poems have a brief introduction, and appear with very full facing vocabulary. Our goal remains, as it was originally, to bring the text of Catullus to a student with a minimum of two years of Latin. Our notes are brief and to the point. They are always aimed at fostering a lucid comprehension of the text under study. A general vocabulary appears at the end of the book and is a collection of all the words we glossed.

A teacher's manual contains a rough translation of each poem and a battery of tests which exercise a student on points of grammar, identification, meter, figures of speech, as well as the translation and comprehension of each poem. Essay questions, modeled on those encountered in A.P. Examinations, are also featured in the Teacher's Manual. A full bibliography on each poem and reproducible pages of the Latin text for each poem complete the Teacher's Edition.

We sincerely hope that our efforts will help foster continued study of Catullus and continued use of the Advanced Placement Examinations in Latin. We would like to thank our publisher Dr. Ladislaus Bolchazy and our editor LeaAnn Osburn for their enthusiastic support of this project. I, Henry Bender, extend special thanks to Professor Blaise Nagy for his guidance through this project, and a particular debt of gratitude to my wife Jane for her support. I, Phyllis Forsyth, thank my husband Jim for his support.

Henry V. Bender, Ph.D.
The Hill School and St. Joseph's University

Phyllis Young Forsyth, Ph.D.
University of Waterloo

Advanced Placement Syllabus
Catullus
2004–2005

DELETIONS:
Old Syllabus Poems Omitted from New Syllabus
9, 27, 34, 53, 62, 73, 75, 83, 92, 95, 107

RETENTIONS:
Old Syllabus Poems Kept in New Syllabus
1, 2, 3, 4, 5, 7, 8, 10, 11, 12, 13, 22, 31, 35, 36,
43, 44, 45, 46, 49, 50, 51, 70, 72, 76, 77, 84,
85, 86, 87, 96, 101, 109

ADDITIONS:
New Poems Added to the Revised Old Syllabus
14a, 30, 40, 60, 64.50-253, 65, 68.1-40, 69, 116

COMPLETE NEW SYLLABUS:
1, 2, 3, 4, 5, 7, 8, 10, 11, 12, 13, 14a, 22, 30, 31,
35, 36, 40, 43, 44, 45, 46, 49, 50, 51, 60,
64 lines 50-253, 65, 68 lines 1-40, 69, 70, 72,
76, 77, 84, 85, 86, 87, 96, 101, 109, 116

14a
Lines 1–15

On the occasion of the feast of Saturnalia, Gaius Licinius Calvus (see poem 50, 53, 96), poet and close friend of Catullus, has sent him a gift for his reading pleasure. However, Catullus' reaction to his receipt of the *libellus* shows extreme displeasure with its contents, since, most likely in keeping with the spirit of the occasion, the poems of the *libellus* are in fact of very poor quality, not at all on the level of the poetry of Catullus or Calvus. The meter is hendecasyllabic.

> Ni te plus oculis meis amarem,
> iucundissime Calve, munere isto
> odissem te odio Vatiniano:
> nam quid feci ego quidve sum locutus,
> cur me tot male perderes poetis?   5
> isti di mala multa dent clienti,
> qui tantum tibi misit impiorum.
> quod si, ut suspicor, hoc novum ac repertum
> munus dat tibi Sulla litterator,
> non est mi male, sed bene ac beate,   10
> quod non dispereunt tui labores.
> di magni, horribilem et sacrum libellum,
> quem tu scilicet ad tuum Catullum
> misti, continuo ut die periret
> Saturnalibus, optimo dierum!   15

1   **Ni=si non,** if not, unless
     oculis meis, ablative of comparison with **plus**

2   **munere: munus, muneris,** n., gift; the gift is the **libellus** (ablative of cause)

3   **odissem: odi, odisse,** hate; in form the pluperfect subjunctive active; **odi** is a defective verb and can be found only in perfect system forms; this is equivalent here to the imperfect subjunctive in a contrary to fact condition.
     odio: odium, odii, n., hatred; note the polyptoton with **odissem**
     Vatiniano: Vatinianus-a-um, adj., pertaining to Publius Vatinius (Poem 53 line 2), associated with Julius Caesar and prosecuted in 54BC by Calvus; hence Calvus would be hated by Vatinius.

4   **sum locutus: loquor, loqui, locutus sum,** speak, say

5   **cur: cur,** conj., why; in this line equivalent to **ut** introducing a result clause
     male: adv., badly, very much, excessively
     perderes: perdo, perdere, perdidi, perditum, lose utterly, destroy
     poetis, ablative with the sense of "with"

6   **isti,** modifies **clienti**; note the chiasmus in this line.
   dent is jussive subjunctive.
   clienti: cliens, clientis, m., client

7   **tantum: tantus-a-um,** adj., so much, so great; accusative neuter object of the verb; here in the sense of "such a mass"
   impiorum: impius-a-um, adj., unworthy, (as a substantive) "wrongdoers" or "scoundrels" (genitive of the whole)

8   **quod si,** but if
   ut: ut, conj., as (followed by the indicative mood)
   suspicor: suspicor, suspicari, suspicatus sum, suspect, suppose, conjecture
   novum...repertum...munus (line 9) are all in the accusative case, objects of the verb **dat.** Note the hendiadys with **novum** and **repertum**
   repertum: reperio, reperire, repperi, repertum, discover; here "devised" (for the Saturnalia)

9   Sulla is not known but is characterized here by the word **litterator,** which denotes a person more concerned with the mechanics of language learning than with any profound aspects of literature; the **litterator** is regarded by Fordyce (136) as "an elementary schoolmaster."

10   Note the use of alliteration in this line.

11   **dispereunt: dispereo, disperire, disperii,** to go to ruin, be undone, perish; the form is an example of the historical present tense.

12   **sacrum: sacer, sacra, sacrum,** adj., sacred, holy; here in the sense of accursed

13   **scilicet: scilicet,** adv., for sure, of course

14   **misti=misisti** (syncope)
   continuo: continuus-a-um, adj., following, probably modifies **die,** but may be an adverb which has the meaning of "on the spot."
   periret, subjunctive in a purpose clause.

15   **Saturnalibus: Saturnalia, Saturnaliorum,** n., festival of the Saturnalia beginning on 17 December, named for the god Saturnus equivalent to the Greek Titan Kronos; this was a festival where *what should not be* was accepted as *what can be,* a feast of reversal, reinforced by gift exchanges among friends, family, and others; **Saturnalibus** is in apposition with **die** (line 14); **optimo** is in apposition to Saturnalibus.

14a
Lines 16–25

non non hoc tibi, salse, sic abibit:
nam, si luxerit, ad librariorum
curram scrinia, Caesios, Aquinos,
Suffenum, omnia colligam venena,
ac te his suppliciis remunerabor.   20
vos hinc interea valete abite
illuc, unde malum pedem attulistis,
saecli incommoda, pessimi poetae

16 **hoc** refers to Calvus' prank of giving such a bad book of poetry to Catullus.
    salse: salsus-a-um, adj., witty, sharp, acute; **salse** is the vocative form directed to Calvus.
    abibit: abeo, abire, abii, come out, come off; here "be allowed to pass" for you (tibi)

17 **luxerit: luceo, lucere, luxi,** be light, be clear, shine; the verb form is future perfect indicative active, but is best translated, "if there will be light at dawn tomorrow."
    librariorum: librarius-a-um, adj., pertaining to books, (as a substantive) transcriber of books

18 **scrinia; scrinium, scrinii,** n., a cylindrical box or case for letters or scrolls; **scrinia** implies (with **librariorum**) a booksellers shop.
    Caesios, Aquinos: plural forms of proper names intended to typify the bad poets whose writings make up the **libellus**

19 **Suffenum: Suffenus, -i,** m., Suffenus, a poet disliked by Catullus (Poem 22)
    colligam: colligo, colligere, collegi, collectum, gather, collect
    venena: venenum, -i, n., poison

20 **suppliciis: supplicium, supplicii,** n., a bowing down, petition, punishment, "instruments of torture" (Forsyth 161); the retribution which Catullus has in mind is the collection of bad poems which he will assemble as a return gift, characterized as **venena** and **supplicia.**
    remunerabor: remuneror, remunerari, remuneratus sum, repay, reward

21 Note the asyndeton with the imperatives in this line reflecting the intensity of the poet's anger.

22 **pedem: pes, pedis,** m., foot; the **pes** is associated with a metrical foot and serves here as a punning reference to the meter, i.e. the poems themselves that Catullus despises. Catullus effectively refers both literally to the departure on foot of the **pessimi poetae** and figuratively to their bad step **(pedem)** into the world of poetry.

23 **saecli=saeculi: saeculum, -i,** n., age, era
    incommoda: incommodum, incommodi, n., trouble, loss, misfortune; **incommoda** is in apposition with the vocative **pessimi poetae.**

30

In addressing a certain Alfenus, perhaps the Varus of poems 10 and 22, Catullus poses four rhetorical questions (lines 1-6) and then offers possible responses (line 7–12). The vocabulary of despair and depression characterizes the poet's collapsed relationship with Alfenus. This is the only poem of the Catullan corpus in the greater Asclepiadean meter.

> Alfene immemor atque unanimis false sodalibus,
> iam te nil miseret, dure, tui dulcis amiculi?
> iam me prodere, iam non dubitas fallere, perfide?
> nec facta impia fallacum hominum caelicolis placent.
> quae tu neglegis, ac me miserum deseris in malis;   5
> eheu quid faciant, dic, homines cuive habeant fidem?
> certe tute iubebas animam tradere, inique, \<me\>
> inducens in amorem, quasi tuta omnia mi forent.
> idem nunc retrahis te ac tua dicta omnia factaque
> ventos irrita ferre ac nebulas aereas sinis.   10
> si tu oblitus es, at di meminerunt, meminit Fides,
> quae te ut paeniteat postmodo facti faciet tui.

1   **immemor: immemor, immemoris,** adj., unmindful; "heedless of obligation"
    unanimis: unanimus-a-um, adj., of one mind, faithful
    false: falsus-a-um, adj., false, disloyal (governs the dative case here)
    sodalibus: sodalis, -is, m., friend, comrade

2   **iam: iam,** adv., now, in the surprised sense of "just now"
    miseret: misereo, miserere, miserui, take pity on, move someone to have pity for or on
        (with genitive case); this impersonal verb takes a direct object and a genitive; here
        "have you no pity at all for…"
    amiculi: the diminutive form of **amicus** reveals the special affection of the poet.

3   **prodere: prodo, prodere, prodidi, proditum,** betray
    fallere: fallo, fallere, fefelli, falsum, deceive

4   **fallacum: fallax, fallacis,** adj., deceitful, deceptive

5   **quae** refers to the sum of all the things referenced or implied by lines 1–4, "all these
        things."
    neglegis: here in the sense of "ignore" or "make light of"

6   **faciant** is subjunctive in indirect question; **homines** is nominative plural.

7   **tute** is the intensive form of **tu.**
    iubebas: iubeo, iubere, iussi, iussum, order, compel
    tradere: trado, tradere, tradidi, traditum, hand over, entrust
    inique: iniquus-a-um, adj., unfair, unjust

8   **amorem,** not sexual but emotional
    forent=essent

9   **retrahis: retraho, retrahere, retraxi, retractum,** draw back

10 **irrita: irritus-a-um,** adj., worthless, unsettled, null and void
    nebulas: nebula, -ae, f., cloud
    aereus-a-um, adj., copper or bronze colored; some texts read **aerius-a-um** here: airy,
        lofty
    sinis: sino, sinere, sivi, situm, permit, allow

11 **oblitus es: obliviscor, oblivisci, oblitus sum,** forget
    at: at, conj., yet
    di=dei
    meminerunt: memini, meminisse, remember

12 **quae** refers to Fides, the cult goddess of Good Faith, and is in the nominative case,
        subject of **faciet.**
    paeniteat: paenitet, paenitere, paenituit, (impersonal verb) it pains; the form is in the
        subjunctive mood in a clause of result introduced by **faciet,** and takes an accusative
        of the person affected (**te**) and a genitive to express the thing causing the affliction
        (**facti**). A literal translation would be "who will bring it about so that it pains you
        shortly of your deed."

40

Apparently the otherwise unknown Ravidus of this poem has dared to make a play for Catullus' beloved Lesbia. This action has therefore drawn the fierce ire of Catullus, who directs a series of rhetorical questions at him (lines 1–6), capped with a promise of future suffering (lines 7–8). The meter is hendecasyllabic.

> Quaenam te mala mens, miselle Ravide,
> agit praecipitem in meos iambos?
> quis deus tibi non bene advocatus
> vecordem parat excitare rixam?
> an ut pervenias in ora vulgi?   5
> quid vis? qualubet esse notus optas?
> eris, quandoquidem meos amores
> cum longa voluisti amare poena.

1   **quaenam: quinam-quaenam-quodnam,** inter. adj., what (a strong interrogative)
miselle: misellus-a-um, adj., wretched, miserable, pathetic
Ravide is vocative and must be pronounced as **Raude**, two syllables not three; this may
     be deliberate by Catullus to mock Ravidus.

2   **iambos: iambus, -i,** m., iambic poetry; refers to Catullus' hostile invectives aimed at
     those who displease him.

3   **quis** is here equivalent to an interrogative adjective modifying **deus.**
advocatus: advoco, advocare, advocavi, advocatum, invoke

4   **vecordem: vecors, vecordis,** adj., senseless, mad, insane
rixam: rixa, rixae, f., brawl, quarrel

5   **pervenias: pervenio, pervenire, perveni, perventum,** reach, come to; **pervenias** is
     subjunctive mood in a purpose clause introduced by the understood verb **fecisti.**
ora: os, oris, n., mouth, lips
vulgi: vulgus, -i, n., crowd, people

6   **qualubet: qualubet=qualibet,** adv., everywhere, where you will, in any way you please

7   **quandoquidem: quandoquidem,** conj., since indeed, seeing that, since
amores: Catullus here uses the plural form to refer to a lover; see also poems 10.1 and
     45.1.

8   The **longa poena** amounts to the continued existence of this poem; essentially, as in
     poem 14, the punishment is poetry, but in this instance the poem itself is the
     punishment.

60

Lacking an addressee, this single sentence poem poses a weighty rhetorical question aimed at the unknown person who has shown an appalling lack of concern for the poet by ignoring the special desperation of the moment and the poet's crying need for attention. The meter is limping iambic (choliambic).

> Num te leaena montibus Libystinis
> aut Scylla latrans infima inguinum parte
> tam mente dura procreavit ac taetra,
> ut supplicis vocem in novissimo casu
> contemptam haberes, a nimis fero corde?　　　　　　5

1 **Num: num** is a particle which expects a negative response.
leaena: leaena, -ae, f., lioness
Libystinis: Libystinus-a-um, adj., African

2 Scylla is the Homeric sea monster whose seaweed-girdled waist conceals six barking dogs, but whose upper body is female. The language of lines 1-3 is very similar to that of 64 lines 154-156.
latrans: latro, latrare, latravi, latratum, bark
infima: infimus-a-um, adj., lowest
inguinum: inguen, inguinis, n., groin

3 **taetra: taeter-taetra-taetrum,** adj., repulsive, offensive

4 **supplicis: supplex, supplicis,** adj., (substantive) a supplicant
novissimo: novissimus-a-um, adj., newest, last, most recent
casu: casus, -us, m., event, misfortune, crisis

5 **contemptam: contemptus-a-um,** adj., despised, despicable
haberes here has the sense of "regard."
a:a, inter., an interjection expressing various feelings such as regret, distress, pity
nimis: nimis, adv., too much, excessively
fero: ferus-a-um, adj., hard, fierce, wild
corde: cor, cordis, n. heart; **a nimis fero corde:** "ah, (you) with a heart much too savage"

64
Lines 50–67

Catullus' most ambitious undertaking, Poem 64 takes the form of an *epyllion*, or small-scale epic, dealing with the myth of the wedding of Peleus and Thetis. Its 408 lines, however, are structured as a "tale within a tale" (ecphrasis) as the story of the wedding is interrupted by an inner tale on the myth of Ariadne and Theseus (lines 50–264, from which this excerpt is taken). The link between the two tales is a marriage couch on view at the wedding: it is adorned with a coverlet on which Ariadne is shown abandoned by Theseus on the deserted island of Dia (perhaps the ancient name of Naxos). The plight of Ariadne is masterfully depicted by Catullus in a style that breaks sharply with his normal "lyric" mode but maintains the emotional quality for which the poet is famous. The meter is dactylic hexameter.

Haec vestis priscis hominum variata figuris	50
heroum mira virtutes indicat arte.	
namque fluentisono prospectans litore Diae,	
Thesea cedentem celeri cum classe tuetur	
indomitos in corde gerens Ariadna furores,	
necdum etiam sese quae visit visere credit,	55
utpote fallaci quae tum primum excita somno	
desertam in sola miseram se cernat harena.	
immemor at iuvenis fugiens pellit vada remis,	
irrita ventosae linquens promissa procellae.	
Quem procul ex alga maestis Minois ocellis,	60
saxea ut effigies bacchantis prospicit, eheu,	
prospicit et magnis curarum fluctuat undis,	
non flavo retinens subtilem vertice mitram,	
non contecta levi velatum pectus amictu,	
non tereti strophio lactentis vincta papillas,	65
omnia quae toto delapsa e corpore passim	
ipsius ante pedes fluctus salis adludebant.	

50   **priscis: priscus-a-um,** adj., ancient, venerable (transferred epithet)
      variata: vario, variare, variavi, variatum, vary; here in the sense of "adorned with"

51   **heroum: heros, herois,** m., hero

52   **fluentisono: fluentisonus-a-um,** adj., resounding with waves
      Diae: Dia, -ae, f., Dia is the name of an island north of Crete; some claim it was the ancient name of the modern island of Naxos.

53 **Thesea:** Theseus, Athenian hero; **Thesea** is a Greek accusative.
   cedentem: cedo, cedere, cessi, cessum, depart, withdraw
   tuetur: tueor, tueri, tuitus sum, watch, see, look at

54 **Ariadna: Ariadna, -ae,** f., daughter of Minos, King of Crete

56 **utpote: utpote,** adv., as is possible, seeing that, in as much as

58 **pellit: pello, pellere, pepuli, pulsum,** beat, strike, push
   vada: vadum, -i, n., sea, water, shoal

59 **irrita: irritus-a-um,** adj., invalid, worthless, null and void
   ventosae: ventosus-a-um, adj., windy, fickle, inconstant

60 **alga: alga, -ae,** f., sea-weed
   Minois: Minois, Minoidis, f., daughter of King Minos of Crete (Ariadne)

61 **saxea: saxeus-a-um,** adj., rocky
   ut: ut, adv., as, just as
   effigies: effigies, -ei, f., statue, image
   bacchantis: bacchor, bacchari, bacchatus sum, to rave like a Bacchant (a wild devotee
       of the god of wine and frenzy, Bacchus)
   eheu: eheu, interj., alas

62 **fluctuat: fluctuo, fluctuare, fluctuavi, fluctuatum,** move in waves, waver, vacillate, toss

63 **flavo: flavus-a-um,** adj., yellow, golden
   subtilem: subtilis, -e, adj., finely woven, dainty, delicate
   vertice: vertex, -icis, m. top, head; here in the sense of "hair" (note the metonymy)
   mitram: mitra, -ae, f., head-dress, bonnet, ceremonial cap or diadem

64 **contecta: contego, contegere, contexi, contectum,** cover, hide, conceal; the perfect
       passive participle governs **pectus** (accusative of respect), as **vincta** governs **papillas**
       (line 65).
   velatum: velo, velare, velavi, velatum, clothe, veil, conceal
   amictu: amictus, -us, m., dress, clothing, garment

65 **tereti: teres, teretis,** adj., elegant, shapely
   strophio: strophium, strophii, n., breast-band
   lactentis: lactens, -entis, adj., milky, milk-white
   vincta: vincio, vincire, vinxi, vinctum, bind
   papillas: papilla, -ae, f., breast

66 **omnia** is in the accusative case, object of the verb **adludebant** (line 67).

67 **adludebant: adludo, adludere, adlusi, adlusum,** play, play with

64
Lines 68–85

ipsius ante pedes fluctus salis adludebant.
sed neque tum mitrae neque tum fluitantis amictus
illa vicem curans toto ex te pectore, Theseu,
toto animo, tota pendebat perdita mente.   70
a misera, assiduis quam luctibus externavit
spinosas Erycina serens in pectore curas,
illa tempestate, ferox quo tempore Theseus
egressus curvis e litoribus Piraei
attigit iniusti regis Gortynia templa.   75
   Nam perhibent olim crudeli peste coactam
Androgeoneae poenas exsolvere caedis
electos iuvenes simul et decus innuptarum
Cecropiam solitam esse dapem dare Minotauro.
quis angusta malis cum moenia vexarentur,   80
ipse suum Theseus pro caris corpus Athenis
proicere optavit potius quam talia Cretam
funera Cecropiae nec funera portarentur.
atque ita nave levi nitens ac lenibus auris
magnanimum ad Minoa venit sedesque superbas.   85

68   **fluitantis: fluito, fluitare, fluitavi, fluitatum**, flow, float

69   **vicem:** the accusative of a defective noun for "change" that in the singular occurs in the genitive and ablative forms only; the accusative form usually is adverbial. Here **vicem** has the meaning of "for" and governs the two genitives in the preceding line.

70   **perdita: perditus-a-um,** adj., desperate, abandoned

71   **a:** ah! (interjection)
   externavit=exsternavit: exsterno, exsternare, exsternavi, exsternatum, terrify, make mad

72 **spinosas: spinosos-a-um,** adj., thorny, difficult
  Erycina: Erycinus-a-um, adj., of or pertaining to Mt. Eryx in Sicily, sacred to Venus, an epithet for Venus
  serens: sero, serere, sevi, satum, sow

73 **tempestate: tempestas, tempestatis,** f., time, the weather, storm; a very general reference to the time of Theseus' legendary escapade to Crete

74 **egressus: egredior, egredi, egressus sum,** go out, put to sea
  Piraei: Piraeus, -i, m., Piraeus, the port of Athens

75 **attigit: attingo, attingere, attigi, attactum,** touch, arrive at
  Gortynia: Gortynius-a-um, adj., Gortynian, from town of Gortyna on Crete
  templa is metonymy for the famous Cretan palace of King Minos.

76 **perhibent: perhibeo, perhibere, perhibui, perhibitum,** assert, call, say
  coactam modifies **Cecropiam** (line 79).

77 **Androgeoneae: Androgeoneus-a-um,** adj., of or pertaining to Androgeus, a son of King Minos, who was murdered by Aegeus, King of Athens, because of the former's constant wrestling victories in Athenian games; Minos besieged Athens and forced Aegeus, father of Theseus, to send annually fourteen Athenian youths (7 boys and 7 girls) to Crete, where they became fodder for the half-bull, half-man cannibal, the Minotaur. This arrangement prevented war between Athens and Crete.
  exsolvere: exsolvo, exsolvere, exsolvi, exsolutum, pay, exact

78 **electos: eligo, eligere, elegi, electum,** choose, pick
  decus: decus, decoris, n., glory, "the flower"

79 **Cecropiam: Cecropius-a-um,** adj., Athenian, from King Cecrops of Athens; **Cecropiam** is used as a substantive here, meaning Athens.
  dapem: daps, dapis, f., religious feast, a sacrificial meal

80 **quis=quibus**
  angusta: angustus-a-um, narrow
  vexarentur: vexo, vexare, vexavi, vexatum, trouble, harass, toss violently

82 **Cretam: Creta, -ae,** f., Crete; here meaning "to Crete" without any preposition

83 **funera: funus, funeris,** n., burial, corpse; **funera...nec funera** gives the sense of living corpses, that is, the living youths are sent to their deaths on Crete. Note the oxymoron.

84 **nitens: nitor, niti, nisus sum,** press onward
  auris: aura, -ae, f., wind, breeze, air

64
Lines 86–109

hunc simul ac cupido conspexit lumine virgo
regia, quam suavis expirans castus odores
lectulus in molli complexu matris alebat,
quales Eurotae progignunt flumina myrtos
aurave distinctos educit verna colores,   90
non prius ex illo flagrantia declinavit
lumina, quam cuncto concepit corpore flammam
funditus atque imis exarsit tota medullis.
heu misere exagitans immiti corde furores
sancte puer, curis hominum qui gaudia misces,   95
quaeque regis Golgos quaeque Idalium frondosum,
qualibus incensam iactastis mente puellam
fluctibus in flavo saepe hospite suspirantem!
quantos illa tulit languenti corde timores!
quanto saepe magis fulgore expalluit auri,   100
cum saevum cupiens contra contendere monstrum
aut mortem appeteret Theseus aut praemia laudis!
non ingrata tamen frustra munuscula divis
promittens tacito succepit vota labello.
nam velut in summo quatientem bracchia Tauro   105
quercum aut conigeram sudanti cortice pinum
indomitus turbo contorquens flamine robur,
eruit (illa procul radicitus exturbata
prona cadit, late quaevis cumque obvia frangens),

86   **simul ac: simul ac,** conj., as soon as
      lumine: lumen, luminis, n., light; here in the sense of "eye"

87   **suavis: suavis, -e,** adj., sweet, delightful
      castus: castus-a-um, adj., pure, chaste, innocent

88   **alebat: alo, alere, alui, altum,** rear, raise

89   **Eurotae: Eurotas, -ae,** m., the Eurotas was a river in southern Greece.
      progignunt: progigno, progignere, progenui, progenitum, beget, produce
      myrtos: myrtus, -i, f., myrtle

90   **verna: vernus-a-um,** adj., of spring

91   **flagrantia: flagrans, flagrantis,** adj., burning, glowing, blazing

93 **funditus: funditus,** adv., utterly, completely
    exarsit: exardesco, exardescere, exarsi, exarsum, blaze out, kindle, take fire
    medullis: medulla, -ae, f., marrow, bone marrow

94 **misere: misere,** adv., wretchedly
    exagitans: exagito, exagitare, exagitavi, exagitatum, incite, disturb, excite
    immiti: immitis, -e, adj., harsh, rude, inexorable

96 **Golgos: Golgi, -orum,** m., Golgi, a site on Cyprus, an island much associated with
        Venus
    Idalium: Idalium, Idalii, n., Idalium, a town on Cyprus also associated with Venus
    frondosum: frondosus-a-um, adj., rich in leaves

97 **iactastis=iactavistis: iacto, iactare, iactavi, iactatum,** throw, toss

98 **flavo: flavus-a-um,** adj., golden, yellow, blonde
    suspirantem: suspiro, suspirare, suspiravi, suspiratum, take a deep breath, heave a
        sigh

99 **languenti: languens, -entis,** adj., faint, weak

100 **quanto:** with magis (ablative of measure of difference)
    fulgore: fulgor, fulgoris, m., glitter, gleam, flash, brightness; ablative of comparison
        with **magis**
    expalluit: expallesco, expallescere, expallui, expallitum, turn pale

103 **munuscula: munusculum, -i,** n., small present

104 **succepit=suscepit: suscipio, suscipere, suscepi, susceptum,** take up, undertake, pledge
    labello: labellum, -i, n., lip

105 **velut: velut,** adv., just as; here it introduces a simile.
    quatientem: quatio, quatere, quassi, quassum, shake
    Tauro: Taurus, Tauri, m., Taurus, a mountain range in southern Asia Minor

106 **quercum: quercus, -us,** f., oak
    conigeram: coniger, conigera, conigerum, adj., cone-bearing
    sudanti: sudo, sudare, sudavi, sudatum, sweat, perspire
    cortice: cortex, corticis, m./f., bark
    pinum: pinus, -i, f., pine

107 **indomitus: indomitus-a-um,** adj., wild
    turbo: turbo, turbinis, m., a whirlwind, tornado
    contorquens: contorqueo, contorquere, contorsi, contortum, twist, turn
    flamine: flamen, flaminis, n., gale, wind
    robur: robur, roboris, n., oak; here in the sense of "the tree trunk"

108 **eruit: eruo, eruere, erui, erutum,** uproot
    radicitus: radicitus, adv., by the roots, utterly
    exturbata: exturbo, exturbare, exturbavi, exturbatum, force out, knock out

109 **prona: pronus-a-um,** adj., leaning forward, headlong, downwards
    quaeviscumque: quiviscumque, quaeviscumque, quodviscumque, adj., any
        whatsoever; this indefinite adjective modifies the neuter substantive **obvia.**
    obvia: obvius-a-um, adj., in the way, so as to meet, meeting; here "whatever is in the
        way"

64
Lines 110–133

sic domito saevum prostravit corpore Theseus 110
nequiquam vanis iactantem cornua ventis.
inde pedem sospes multa cum laude reflexit
errabunda regens tenui vestigia filo,
ne labyrintheis e flexibus egredientem
tecti frustraretur inobservabilis error. 115
   Sed quid ego a primo digressus carmine plura
commemorem, ut linquens genitoris filia vultum,
ut consanguineae complexum, ut denique matris,
quae misera in gnata deperdita laeta\<batur>,
omnibus his Thesei dulcem praeoptarit amorem: 120
aut ut vecta rati spumosa ad litora Diae,
\<venerit> aut ut eam devinctam lumina somno
liquerit immemori discedens pectore coniunx?
saepe illam perhibent ardenti corde furentem
clarisonas imo fudisse e pectore voces, 125
ac tum praeruptos tristem conscendere montes,
unde aciem \<in> pelagi vastos protenderet aestus,
tum tremuli salis adversas procurrere in undas
mollia nudatae tollentem tegmina surae,
atque haec extremis maestam dixisse querellis, 130
frigidulos udo singultus ore cientem:
   "Sicine me patriis avectam, perfide, ab aris,
perfide, deserto liquisti in litore, Theseu?

---

110 **domito: domo, domare, domui, domitum,** tame, conquer, break, subdue

111 **vanis: vanus-a-um,** adj. safe, unhurt

112 **sospes: sospes, sospitis,** adj., safe, unhurt
reflexit: reflecto, reflectere, reflexi, reflexum, turn back, turn about

113 **errabunda: errabundus-a-um,** adj., wandering
regens: rego, regere, rexi, rectum, direct, guide, steer
vestigia: vestigium, vestigii, n., footstep
filo: filum, -i, n., thread, string

114 **labyrintheis: labyrintheus-a-um,** adj., labyrinthine, twisted, contorted
flexibus: flexus, -us, m., winding

115 **frustraretur: frustror, frustrari, frustratus sum,** trick, deceive
inobservabilis: inobservabilis, -e, adj., unnoticed, untraceable
error: error, erroris, m., maze, wandering

116 **ego**=the poet
carmina: carmen, -inis. n., song; here "storyline." Lines 116–123 bring the reader back to Anadne an the shore (line 70).

117 **commemorem: commemoro, commemorare, commemoravi, commemoratum,** relate, recall

119 **misera** foreshadows the future misery of Ariadne.
gnata=nata: nata, -ae, f., daughter
deperdita: deperdo, deperdere, deperdidi, deperditum, ruin, destroy
laetabatur: laetor, laetari, laetatus sum, rejoice, take delight; here "used to take delight"

120 **praeoptarit=praeoptaverit:** **praeopto, praeoptare, praeoptavi, praeoptatum,** prefer

121 **ratis: ratis, -is,** f., boat

122 **devinctam: devincio, devincire, devinxi, devinctum,** bind; as in line 64, the perfect participle here virtually takes **lumina** as its object, although **lumina** is best understood as an accusative of respect.

123 **coniunx**=Theseus

124 **perhibent: perhibeo, perhibere, perhibui, perhibitum,** assert, call

125 **clarisonas: clarisonus-a-um,** adj., clear sounding, loud and clear
fudisse: fundo, fundere, fudi, fusum, pour, shed, utter

126 **praeruptos: praeruptus-a-um,** adj., sheer, steep
tristem: tristis, -e, adj., sad, mournful
conscendere: the poet changes tense from perfect (**fudisse**) to present, thus giving us a more immediate mental image of Ariadne; he will return to the perfect tense in line 130 (**dixisse).**

127 **aciem: acies, -ei,** f., gaze, sight
aestus: aestus, -us, m., tide, surge of the sea

128 **tremuli: tremulus-a-um,** adj., rippling, trembling

129 **mollia: mollis, -e,** adj., fine, soft, gentle
tegmina: tegmen, tegminis, n., covering
surae: sura, -ae, f., calf (of the leg)

130 **querellis: querella, -ae,** f., lamentation, complaint

131 **frigidulos: frigidulus-a-um,** adj., chilly
udo: udus-a-um, adj., wet
singultus: singultus, -us, m., sob, gasp
cientem: cieo, ciere, civi, citum, call forth, invoke

132 **sicine: sicine,** adv., thus?, so?, is this how?

133 **perfide:** note the anaphora.

64
Lines 134–157

sicine discedens neglecto numine divum,
immemor a! devota domum periuria portas? 135
nullane res potuit crudelis flectere mentis
consilium? tibi nulla fuit clementia praesto,
immite ut nostri vellet miserescere pectus?
at non haec quondam blanda promissa dedisti
voce mihi; non haec miserae sperare iubebas, 140
sed conubia laeta, sed optatos hymenaeos,
quae cuncta aerii discerpunt irrita venti.
nunc iam nulla viro iuranti femina credat,
nulla viri speret sermones esse fideles;
quis dum aliquid cupiens animus praegestit apisci, 145
nil metuunt iurare, nihil promittere parcunt:
sed simul ac cupidae mentis satiata libido est,
dicta nihil metuere, nihil periuria curant.
certe ego te in medio versantem turbine leti
eripui, et potius germanum amittere crevi, 150
quam tibi fallaci supremo in tempore dessem.
pro quo dilaceranda feris dabor alitibusque
praeda, neque iniacta tumulabor mortua terra.
quaenam te genuit sola sub rupe leaena?
quod mare conceptum spumantibus exspuit undis, 155
quae Syrtis, quae Scylla rapax, quae vasta Charybdis,
talia qui reddis pro dulci praemia vita?

135 **devota: devotus-a-um,** adj., accursed
periuria: periurium, periurii, n., perjury, lie; here "lies."

137 **consilium: consilium, consilii,** n., decision, plan
praesto: praesto, adv., at hand, ready

138 **immite: immitis, -e,** adj., severe, inexorable
nostri=poetic plural
miserescere: miseresco, miserescere, feel pity for (with the genitive)

139 **blanda: blandus-a-um,** adj., smooth, charming

140 **non haec:** note the anaphora and the double antithesis with line 139.
   miserae: dative to agree with **mihi** instead of the expected accusative with **iubebas**

142 **aerii: aerius-a-um,** adj., lofty
   discerpunt: discerpo, discerpere, discerpsi, discerptum, disperse, tear apart
   irrita: irritus-a-um, adj., unsettled, invalid; here "null and void"
145 **quis=quibus** (dative of reference)
   praegestit: praegestio, praegestire, be very eager, desire
   apisci: apiscor, apisci, aptus sum, obtain, get

146 **iurare: iuro, iurare, iuravi, iuratum,** swear
   parcunt: parco, parcere, peperci, parsum, refrain from, spare

147 **satiata: satio, satiare, satiavi, satiatum,** satisfy, fill
   libido: libido, libidinis, f., desire, passion

148 **metuere=metuerunt;** the syncopated perfect form seems oddly placed so soon after
   metuunt and so close to **curant;** if the manuscript reading is correct, the perfect
   tense here denotes a lasting result and should be translated as if it was a present
   tense form. Some editors, however, print **meminere** here: "they remember not at all
   their words."

150 **potius: potius,** adv., rather, more
   germanum: germanus, -i, m., brother (the Minotaur)
   crevi: cerno, cernere, crevi, cretum, decide

151 **supremo in tempore:** "in (your) time of greatest need"
   dessem=deessem: desum, deesse, defui, fail (with the dative case)

152 **dilaceranda: dilacero, dilacerare, dilaceravi, dilaceratum,** tear to pieces
   feris: ferus, -i, m., beast
   alitibusque: ales, alitis, f., bird

153 **iniacta=iniecta: inicio, inicere, inieci, iniectum,** throw on
   tumulabor: tumulo, tumulare, tumulavi, tumulatum, bury

154 **quaenam: quinam-quaenam-quodnam,** inter. pro./adj., who then?, who in the world?,
   what?
   leaena: leaena, -ae, f., lioness

155 **conceptum: concipio, concipere, concepi, conceptum,** conceive
   exspuit: exspuo, exspuere, exspui, exsputum, spit out

156 **Syrtis: Syrtis, -is,** f., the Syrtis, a sandbank located on the Gulf of Sidra in North
   Africa, an exotic location dangerous and hostile to all ships
   Scylla: Scylla, -ae, f., Scylla, a monster found in the Straits of Messina, across from
   the location occupied by Charybdis
   Charybdis: Charybdis, -is, f., Charybdis, a monster in the Straits of Messina, often depicted as
   a whirlpool; note the tricolon in this line.

64
Lines 158–177

si tibi non cordi fuerant conubia nostra,
saeva quod horrebas prisci praecepta parentis,
attamen in vestras potuisti ducere sedes,   160
quae tibi iucundo famularer serva labore,
candida permulcens liquidis vestigia lymphis,
pupureave tuum consternens veste cubile.
  Sed quid ego ignaris nequiquam conquerar auris,
externata malo, quae nullis sensibus auctae   165
nec missas audire queunt nec reddere voces?
ille autem prope iam mediis versatur in undis,
nec quisquam apparet vacua mortalis in alga.
sic nimis insultans extremo tempore saeva
fors etiam nostris invidit questibus auris.   170
   Iuppiter omnipotens, utinam ne tempore primo
Cnosia Cecropiae tetigissent litora puppes,
indomito nec dira ferens stipendia tauro
perfidus in Creta religasset navita funem,
nec malus hic celans dulci crudelia forma   175
consilia in nostris requiesset sedibus hospes!
nam quo me referam? Quali spe perdita nitor?

159 **praecepta: praeceptum, -i,** n., order, command

160 **attamen: attamen,** conj., even so, nevertheless

161 **famularer: famulor, famulari, famulatus sum,** serve; subjunctive in a relative clause of purpose

162 **permulcens: permulceo, permulcere, permulsi, permulsum,** rub, soothe
liquidis: liquidus- a-um, adj., pure, clean
vestigia: vestigium, vestigii, n., footprint; "foot" by metonymy
lymphis: lympha, -ae, f., water

163 **consternens: consterno, consternere, constravi, constratum,** cover
cubile: cubile, -is, n., bed, couch, resting place

164 **conquerar: conqueror, conqueri, conquestus sum,** complain, bewail
auris: aura, -ae, f., wind, air, breeze

165 **externata=exsternata: exsterno, exsternare, exsternavi, exsternatum,** terrify greatly
malo: malum, -i, n., evil, woe, misfortune
auctae: augeo, augere, auxi, auctum, increase, enlarge, bless (endow) with

166 **missas: mitto, mittere, misi, missum,** send; here in the sense of "uttered"
queunt: queo, quire, quivi, quitum, be able, can

167 **ille**=Theseus
prope: prope, adv., near
versatur: verso, versare, versavi, versatum, turn; here in the sense of "be situated."
Note the chiasmus in this line.

169 **insultans: insulto, insultare, insultavi, insultatum,** exult

170 **fors: fors, fortis,** f., chance, luck
invidit: invideo, invidere, invidi, invisum, begrudge
questibus: questus, -us, m., complaint, lament
auris=aures: auris, -is, f., ear

172 **Cnosia=Gnosia: Gnosius-a-um,** adj., of or belonging to Knossos, Cretan
Cecropiae: Cecropius-a-um, adj., Athenian (also line 79)
tetigissent: tango, tangere, tetigi, tactum, touch, reach

173 **indomito: indomitus-a-um,** adj., wild, untamed
stipendia: stipendium, stipendii, n., tribute
tauro: taurus, -i, m., bull; here the Minotaur

174 **religasset=religavisset: religo, religare, religavi, religatum,** moor, tie up
navita=nauta: nauta, -ae, m., sailor
funem: funis, -is, m., rope

176 **requiesset=requievisset: requiesco, requiescere, requievi, requietum,** take rest, rest, find rest

177 **perdita: perditus-a-um,** adj., lost, desperate, hopeless, abandoned
nitor: nitor, niti, nisus sum, depend on

64
Lines 178–201

Idaeosne petam montes? At gurgite lato
discernens ponti truculentum dividit aequor.
an patris auxilium sperem? Quemne ipsa reliqui,   180
respersum iuvenem fraterna caede secuta?
coniugis an fido consoler memet amore?
quine fugit lentos incurvans gurgite remos?
praeterea nullo colitur sola insula tecto,
nec patet egressus pelagi cingentibus undis.   185
nulla fugae ratio, nulla spes: omnia muta,
omnia sunt deserta, ostentant omnia letum.
non tamen ante mihi languescent lumina morte,
nec prius a fesso secedent corpore sensus,
quam iustam a divis exposcam prodita multam   190
caelestumque fidem postrema comprecer hora.
 "Quare facta virum multantes vindice poena,
Eumenides, quibus anguino redimita capillo
frons expirantis praeportat pectoris iras,
huc huc adventate, meas audite querellas,   195
quas ego, vae misera, extremis proferre medullis
cogor inops, ardens, amenti caeca furore.
quae quoniam verae nascuntur pectore ab imo,
vos nolite pati nostrum vanescere luctum,
sed quali solam Theseus me mente reliquit,   200
tali mente, deae, funestet seque suosque."

178 **Idaeos: Idaeus-a-um,** adj., pertaining to the Ida mountain range on Crete

179 **discernens: discerno, discernere, discrevi, discretum,** separate
truculentum: truculentus-a-um, adj., wild, grim

181 **respersum: respergo, respergere, respersi, respersum,** stain

182 **consoler: consolor, consolari, consolatus sum,** console, comfort, cheer
memet=me

183 **lentos: lentus-a-um,** adj., tough, pliable
incurvans: incurvo, incurvare, incurvavi, incurvatum, bend

184 **colitur: colo, colere, colui, cultum,** inhabit
sola here means "forsaken."

185 **patet: pateo, patere, patui,** be open, lie open, stand open
cingentibus: cingo, cingere, cinxi, cinctum, surround, enclose; **cingentibus undis** is an
ablative absolute.

186 **ratio: ratio, rationis,** f. way, method, procedure, reason, cause

187 **ostentant: ostento, ostentare, ostentavi, ostentatum,** present to view, show, exhibit, hold
out

188 **languescent: languesco, languescere, langui,** weaken, grow faint

189 **prius** with **quam** in line 190 is an example of tmesis, **priusquam.**
secedent: secedo, secedere, secessi, secessum, withdraw, retire

190 **prodita: prodo, prodere, prodidi, proditum,** give up, surrender, abandon, betray
multam: multa, -ae, f., penalty

191 **comprecer: comprecor, comprecari, comprecatus sum,** implore, supplicate

192 **multantes: multo, multare, multavi, multatum,** punish
vindice: vindex, vindicis, m./f., protector, deliverer, avenger; (here used adjectivally)
"avenging"

193 **Eumenides: Eumenides, Eumenidum,** f., the Furies, the avenging goddesses with snakes
in their hair
quibus is dative of possession
anguino: anguinus-a-um, adj., snaky
redimita: redimio, redimire, redimii, redimitum, crown, encircle
capillo: capillus, -i, m., hair

194 **expirantis=exspirantes: exspiro, exspirare, exspiravi, exspiratum,** breathe out, rush
out
praeportat: praeporto, praeportare, praeportavi, praeportatum, manifest, carry before

195 **adventate: advento, adventare, adventavi, adventatum,** come in haste, advance

196 **medullis: medulla, -ae,** f., marrow; here in the sense of "heart"

197 **inops: inops, inopis,** adj., without resources, helpless

198 **quoniam: quoniam,** conj., since now, whereas

199 **pati: patior, pati, passus sum,** allow, permit
vanescere: vanesco, vanescere, vanescui, come to nothing, disappear, pass away

201 **funestet: funesto, funestare, funestavi, funestatum,** desecrate, stain with blood

64
Lines 202–227

Has postquam maesto profudit pectore voces,
supplicium saevis exposcens anxia factis,
annuit invicto caelestum numine rector;
quo motu tellus atque horrida contremuerunt   205
aequora concussitque micantia sidera mundus.
ipse autem caeca mentem caligine Theseus
consitus oblito dimisit pectore cuncta,
quae mandata prius constanti mente tenebat,
dulcia nec maesto sustollens signa parenti   210
sospitem Erectheum se ostendit visere portum.
  Namque ferunt olim, classi cum moenia divae
linquentem gnatum ventis concrederet Aegeus,
talia complexum iuveni mandata dedisse:
  "Gnate mihi longa iucundior unice vita,   215
gnate, ego quem in dubios cogor dimittere casus,
reddite in extrema nuper mihi fine senectae,
quandoquidem fortuna mea ac tua fervida virtus
eripit invito mihi te, cui languida nondum
lumina sunt gnati cara saturata figura,   220
non ego te gaudens laetanti pectore mittam,
nec te ferre sinam fortunae signa secundae,
sed primum multas expromam mente querellas,
canitiem terra atque infuso pulvere foedans,
inde infecta vago suspendam lintea malo,   225
nostros ut luctus nostraeque incendia mentis
carbasus obscurata dicet ferrugine Hibera.

203 **anxia: anxius-a-um,** adj., troubled

204 **annuit=adnuit: adnuo, adnuere, adnui, adnutum,** assent, promise
rector: rector, rectoris, m., master; here Zeus/Jupiter

205 **contremuerunt: contremo, contremere, contremui,** tremble, quake

207 **caligine: caligo, caliginis,** f., mist, fog

208 **consitus: consero, conserere, consevi, consitum,** cover, plant, sow

209 **mandata: mandatum, -i,** n., command

210 **sustollens: sustollo, sustollere,** raise, lift up

211 **Erectheum=Erec(h)theus-a-um,** adj., Athenian, from the name of Erechtheus, a legendary King of Athens

212 **classi=classe**
moenia divae refers to the walls of Athens as **divae** means Athena.

213 **gnatum=natum: natus-a-um,** adj., born; here used substantively as "son"
Aegeus: Aegeus, -i, m., Aegeus, father of Theseus, King of Athens

214 **complexum: complector, complecti, complexus sum,** embrace, clasp

215 **unice: unicus-a-um,** adj., one and only

217 **nuper: nuper,** adv., recently
fine: here a feminine noun
senectae: senecta, -ae, f., old age

218 **quandoquidem: quandoquidem,** conj., since indeed, seeing that, since
fervida: fervidus-a-um, adj., fiery

219 **languida: languidus-a-um,** adj., feeble, faint

220 **saturata: saturo, saturare, saturavi, saturatum,** fill, satisfy

222 **sinam: sino, sinere, sivi, situm,** let, allow
secundae: secundus-a-um, adj., favorable, good

223 **expromam: expromo, expromere, exprompsi, expromptum,** state, disclose, bring out
querellas: querella, -ae, f., complaint

224 **canitiem: canities, -ei,** f., grey hair
infuso: infundo, infundere, infudi, infusum, pour on
foedans: foedo, foedare, foedavi, foedatum, befoul, mar, sully

225 **infecta: inficio, inficere, infeci, infectum,** dye, discolor
vago: vagus-a-um, adj., wandering
suspendam: suspendo, suspendere, suspendi, suspensum, hang
lintea: linteum, -i, n., sail
malo: malus, -i, m., mast

226 **luctus: luctus, -us,** m., mourning, lamentation

227 **carbasus: carbasus, -i,** f., sail
obscurata: obscuro, obscurare, obscuravi, obscuratum, darken
ferrugine: ferrugo, ferruginis, f., rust, dark color
Hibera: Hiberus-a-um, adj., Spanish

64
Lines 228–250

quod tibi si sancti concesserit incola Itoni,
quae nostrum genus ac sedes defendere Erecthei
annuit, ut tauri respergas sanguine dextram,   230
tum vero facito ut memori tibi condita corde
haec vigeant mandata, nec ulla oblitteret aetas;
ut simul ac nostros invisent lumina collis,
funestam antennae deponant undique vestem,
candidaque intorti sustollant vela rudentes,   235
quam primum cernens ut laeta gaudia mente
agnoscam, cum te reducem aetas prospera sistet."
   Haec mandata prius constanti mente tenentem
Thesea ceu pulsae ventorum flamine nubes
aereum nivei montis liquere cacumen.   240
at pater, ut summa prospectum ex arce petebat,
anxia in assiduos absumens lumina fletus,
cum primum infecti conspexit lintea veli,
praecipitem sese scopulorum e vertice iecit,
amissum credens immiti Thesea fato.   245
sic funesta domus ingressus tecta paterna
morte ferox Theseus, qualem Minoidi luctum
obtulerat mente immemori, talem ipse recepit.
quae tum prospectans cedentem maesta carinam
multiplices animo volvebat saucia curas.   250

228 **concesserit: concedo, concedere, concessi, concessum,** allow, grant
Itoni: Itonus, Itoni, f., Itonus, a town in Greece sacred to Athena, goddess of Athens
incola Itoni=Athena

230 **respergas: respergo, respergere, respersi, respersum,** sprinkle, stain

231 **facito: facio, facere, feci, factum,** make, do (future imperative form)
condita: condo, condere, condidi, conditum, preserve, store, write

232 **vigeant: vigeo, vigere, vigui,** thrive, live on
mandata: mandatum, -i, n., command
oblitteret: oblittero, oblitterare, oblitteravi, oblitteratum, erase
aetas: aetas, aetatis, f., time

233 **invisent: inviso, invisere, invisi, invisum,** look upon, see
collis: collis, -is, m., hill

234 **funestam: funestus-a-um,** adj., sorrowful
antennae: antenna, -ae, f., the yardarm of a ship

235 **intorti: intortus-a-um,** adj., twisted
sustollant: sustollo, sustollere, raise
rudentes: rudens, rudentis, m., rope, (in the plural) rigging

236 **quam primum: quam primum,** adv., as soon as possible
cernens: cerno, cernere, crevi, cretum, see

237 **agnoscam: agnosco, agnoscere, agnovi, agnitum,** know once more
reducem: redux, reducis, adj., brought back, returned
aetas=tempus here
prospera: prosperus-a-um, adj., fortunate, favorable, successful
sistet: sisto, sistere, stiti, statum, present, produce

239 **ceu: ceu,** adv., just as

240 **aereum: aereus-a-um,** adj., of copper or bronze; some read **aerius-a-um** here: lofty
nivei: niveus-a-um, adj., snowy
liquere=liquerunt: linquo, linquere, liqui, leave, quit
cacumen: cacumen, cacuminis, n., summit

241 **prospectum: prospectus, -us,** m., sight, view

242 **anxia: anxius-a-um,** adj., troubled
assiduos=adsiduos: adsiduus-a-um, adj., incessant
absumens: absumo, absumere, absumpsi, absumptum, exhaust, consume
fletus: fletus, -us, m., weeping, tears; note the alliteration and metonymy in this line.

243 **cum primum: cum primum,** adv., as soon as
veli: velum, -i, n., sail

244 **praecipitem: praeceps, praecipitis,** adj., headfirst

245 **immiti: immitis, -e,** adj., severe, inexorable

246 **funesta: funestus-a-um,** adj., deadly, fatal, in mourning; take with **tecta.**
paterna: paternus-a-um, adj., paternal; take with **morte.**

247 **Minoidi: Minois, Minoidis,** f., daughter of Minos (Ariadne), a Greek dative here

249 **prospectans: prospecto, prospectare, prospectavi, prospectatum,** look out, view
carinam: carina, -ae, f., ship

250 **multiplices: multiplex, multiplicis,** adj., manifold, various

64
Lines 251–253

At parte ex alia florens volitabat Iacchus
cum thiaso Satyrorum et Nysigenis Silenis,
te quaerens, Ariadna, tuoque incensus amore.

251 **florens: florens, florentis,** adj., blooming, shining, bright, youthful
volitabat: volito, volitare, volitavi, volitatum, fly about, flutter, move quickly
Iacchus: Iacchus, -i, m., Bacchus

252 **thiaso: thiasus, -i,** m., a band of dancers
Satyrorum: Satyrus, -i, m., a Satyr, a forest god associated with Bacchus and having
goat's feet
Nysigenis: Nysigena, -ae, m., born on Mount Nysa (birthplace of Bacchus); here used
adjectivally
Silenis: Silenus, -i, m., Sileni, a class of wood-spirits associated with Bacchus

253 **tuo:** take with **amore** as "love for you."

65
Lines 1–9

Addressed to Hortalus, the rival of Cicero, this poem serves as an introduction to poem 66, the translation of Callimachus' *Lock of Berenice*, which Hortalus had requested from Catullus. Catullus explains how the recent death of his brother has severely affected him, ultimately comparing his forgetfulness to the quick embarrassment of a girl who is startled by the sudden appearance of her mother and, as she stands up, an apple, sent to her by her lover, rolls from her lap onto the floor; she blushes as does Catullus. The meter is elegiac distich, the meter of the rest of the corpus, poems 66–116.

Etsi me assiduo confectum cura dolore
sevocat a doctis, Hortale, virginibus,
nec potis est dulcis Musarum expromere fetus
mens animi (tantis fluctuat ipsa malis:
namque mei nuper Lethaeo gurgite fratris   5
pallidulum manans alluit unda pedem,
Troia Rhoeteo quem subter litore tellus
ereptum nostris obterit ex oculis—

1   **assiduo: assiduus-a-um,** adj., continually present, constant
       confectum: conficio, conficere, confeci, confectum, complete; the past participle here means "exhausted."

2   **sevocat: sevoco, sevocare, sevocavi, sevocatum,** separate, call away
       doctis…virginibus are the Muses.
       Hortale=Hortalus, Quintus Hortensius Hortalus (114–50BC), who has apparently asked Catullus for his translation of Callimachus' poem *The Lock of Berenice* (Poem 66)

3   **expromere: expromo, expromere, exprompsi, expromptum,** show forth, display, bring forth
       fetus: fetus, fetus, m., offspring; **fetus** here represents poetry that Catullus can produce at this sad moment in his life, as he explains parenthetically in lines 4–14.

4   **mens animi:** "the mind of my soul," an archaic expression for "mind"
       fluctuat: fluctuo, flutuare, fluctuavi, fluctuatum, flow in waves, toss
       ipsa=mens

5   **Lethaeo gurgite** refers to the Lethe, the river of forgetfulness in Hades, thus representing death.

6   **pallidulum: pallidulus-a-um,** adj., rather dim, pale
       manans: mano, manare, manavi, manatum, flow
       alluit=adluit: adluo, adluere, adlui, flow near to, wash over

7   **Rhoeteo: Rhoeteus-a-um,** adj., of the promontory of Rhoeteum, near Troy
       subter: subter, preposition (with ablative), below, underneath, close to
       Note the chiasmus, found in lines 5–7.

8   **obterit: obtero, obterere, obtrivi, obtritum,** crush, trample

9   This line is missing in manuscripts of the Catullan corpus.

65
Lines 10–24

numquam ego te, vita frater amabilior,   10
aspiciam posthac? at certe semper amabo,
 semper maesta tua carmina morte canam,
qualia sub densis ramorum concinit umbris
 Daulias absumpti fata gemens Ityli):
sed tamen in tantis maeroribus, Hortale, mitto 15
 haec expressa tibi carmina Battiadae,
ne tua dicta vagis nequiquam credita ventis
 effluxisse meo forte putes animo,
ut missum sponsi furtivo munere malum
 procurrit casto virginis e gremio,   20
quod miserae oblitae molli sub veste locatum,
 dum adventu matris prosilit, excutitur;
atque illud prono praeceps agitur decursu,
 huic manat tristi conscius ore rubor.

10 **vita** is ablative of comparison.

11 **posthac: posthac,** adv., in the future, hereafter

12 **tua** modifies **morte**; every subsequent poem in the Catullan corpus is in the elegiac distich, a meter which conveys sorrow (**maesta. . .carmina**) most effectively for Catullus.

13 **qualia: qualis, -e,** adj., just as, just like (understand **carmina**)
concinit: concino, concinere, concinui, sound, sing

14 **Daulias: Daulias, Dauliadis,** adj., of or pertaining to Daulis; here "the Daulian woman"; Daulis was a territory of central Greece ruled by Tereus, husband of Procne and father of her son Itys (here Itylus); Procne kills Itys to punish Tereus for his rape of her sister Philomela; Tereus pursues the sisters, whom the gods metamorphose; Procne becomes a nightingale and Philomela a swallow. This account follows Ovid's version of the myth although there are earlier versions which reverse the roles of Procne and Philomela.

15 **maeroribus: maeror, maeroris,** m., sadness, mourning

16 **expressa: exprimo, exprimere, expressi, expressum,** translate
Battiadae: a reference to the Hellenistic poet Callimachus of Cyrene with whom Catullus has associated himself (compare Poems 7 line 6 and 116 line 2); Battus was the legendary founder of Cyrene, and "Battiades" would mean "inhabitant of Cyrene."

17 **vagis: vagus-a-um,** adj., wandering, rambling, fickle
18 **putes: puto, putare, putavi, putatus,** think; subjunctive in a negative clause of purpose
animo, ablative of separation

19 **ut: ut,** conj., as (followed by the indicative mood), introduces a simile here.
sponsi: sponsus, -i, m., lover, bridegroom
furtivo: furtivus-a-um, adj., stolen, secret
malum: malum, -i, n., apple

20 **gremio: gremium, gremii,** n., lap

21 **quod=malum**
oblitae: oblitus-a-um, adj., forgetful

22 **prosilit: prosilio, prosilire, prosilui,** jump up
excutitur: excutio, excutere, excussi, excussum, shake out

23 **illud=malum**
decursu: decursus, -us, m., descent, fall; note the dominance of spondees in this line, which reflects the girl's sad dismay at the fall of the apple: her secret is out.

24 **conscius: conscius-a-um,** adj., knowing, guilty
rubor: rubor, ruboris, n., blush

68
Lines 1–18

Many scholars feel that this poem is really two poems, 68a (lines 1–40) and 68b (lines 41–160); 68b is omitted from the AP syllabus). It has been suggested that 68a should be seen as an introduction to 68b. However, lines 1–40 do form a coherent structural whole, and can stand legitimately by themselves as a single, self-contained poem. Lines 1–14 function as an introduction; lines 15–26 relate Catullus' reaction to his brother's death as a basis for lines 27–40, which constitute a formal apology to Manlius for Catullus' failure to deliver promised or awaited poems. As was the case in poem 65, the death of his brother has had a terrible effect on the poet. The meter is elegiac distich.

> quod mihi fortuna casuque oppressus acerbo
>   conscriptum hoc lacrimis mittis epistolium,
> naufragum ut eiectum spumantibus aequoris undis
>   sublevem et a mortis limine restituam,
> quem neque sancta Venus molli requiescere somno   5
>   desertum in lecto caelibe perpetitur,
> nec veterum dulci scriptorum carmine Musae
>   oblectant, cum mens anxia pervigilat;
> id gratum est mihi, me quoniam tibi dicis amicum,
>   muneraque et Musarum hinc petis et Veneris;   10
> sed tibi ne mea sint ignota incommoda, Manli,
>   neu me odisse putes hospitis officium,
> accipe, quis merser fortunae fluctibus ipse,
>   ne amplius a misero dona beata petas.
> tempore quo primum vestis mihi tradita pura est,   15
>   iucundum cum aetas florida ver ageret,
> multa satis lusi: non est dea nescia nostri,
>   quae dulcem curis miscet amaritiem;

1   **quod:** "the fact that"
    fortuna casuque, an example of hendiadys
    oppressus: opprimo, opprimere, oppressi, oppressum, crush

2   **conscriptum: conscribo, conscribere, conscripsi, conscriptum,** write
    epistolium: epistolium, epistolii, n., short letter (a diminutive form associated with epistula)

3   **naufragum: naufragus, -i,** m., a shipwrecked man
    eiectum: eicio, eicere, eieci, eiectum, run aground

4   **sublevem: sublevo, sublevare, sublevavi, sublevatum,** lift up

5   **requiescere: requiesco, requiescere, requievi, requietum,** rest, repose

6   **desertum: desertus-a-um,** adj., abandoned, left alone
    caelibe=caelibi: caelebs, caelibis, adj., unmarried, single
    perpetitur: perpetior, perpeti, perpessus sum, endure, permit, allow

8   **oblectant: oblecto, oblectare, oblectavi, oblectatum,** delight, please
    pervigilat: pervigilo, pervigilare, pervigilavi, pervigilatum, stay awake all night

9   **quoniam: quoniam,** conj., since; functions as a subordinate conjunction

10   **hinc: hinc,** adv., from here; meaning "from Catullus" in this context

11   **incommode: incommodus-a-um,** adj., troublesome, (substantively) troubles, misfortunes
    Manli=Manlius; whether this is also the Allius of 68b is contentious.

12   **odisse** literally denotes hate, but here, more appropriately, has the sense of "see no use in" or "have no use for" (Fordyce 345) or "have no concern for" or simply "dislike."
    hospitis: hospes, hospitis, m., guest, host
    officium: officium, officii, n., duty, obligation

13   **accipe: accipio, accipere, accepi, acceptum,** receive, hear
    quis=quibus, modifies **fluctibus**
    merser: merso, mersare, mersavi, mersatum, dip, immerse, overwhelm

14   **amplius: amplius,** adv., any longer
    petas, subjunctive in a negative clause of purpose

15   **pura: purus-a-um,** adj., pure; here "white"; the pure white *toga virilis* was assumed at the age of 16 years and replaced the purple bordered *toga praetexta;* **vestis** is equivalent to **toga** here.

16   **aetas: aetas, aetatis,** f., life
    florida: floridus-a-um, adj., blooming, beautiful; **aetas florida** means "flower of my youth"
    ver: ver, veris, n., spring
    ageret: ago, agere, egi, actum, drive do; here "pass"

17   **multa satis lusi:** these words can mean either that the poet has conducted (**lusi**) enough (**satis**) numerous affairs (**multa**) or has had his fill (**satis**) of composing many poems (**multa**) in a light hearted way (**lusi**).
    dea=Venus
    nostri=mei

18   **amaritiem: amarities, -ei,** f., bitterness

68
Lines 19–40

sed totum hoc studium luctu fraterna mihi mors
    abstulit. o misero frater adempte mihi,   20
tu mea tu moriens fregisti commoda, frater,
    tecum una tota est nostra sepulta domus,
omnia tecum una perierunt gaudia nostra,
    quae tuus in vita dulcis alebat amor.
cuius ego interitu tota de mente fugavi   25
    haec studia atque omnes delicias animi.
quare, quod scribes Veronae turpe Catullo
    esse, quod hic quisquis de meliore nota
frigida deserto tepefactet membra cubili,
    id, Manli, non est turpe, magis miserum est.   30
ignosces igitur, si, quae mihi luctus ademit,
    haec tibi non tribuo munera, cum nequeo.
nam, quod scriptorum non magna est copia apud me,
    hoc fit, quod Romae vivimus: illa domus,
illa mihi sedes, illic mea carpitur aetas: 35
    huc una ex multis capsula me sequitur.
quod cum ita sit, nolim statuas nos mente maligna
    id facere aut animo non satis ingenuo,
quod tibi non utriusque petenti copia posta est:
    ultro ego deferrem, copia siqua foret.   40

19   **studium**: this refers to Catullus' enthusiasm or pursuit.

21   **fregisti: frango, frangere, fregi, fractum,** break
     commoda: commodum, -i, n., advantage; here "everything good"

22   **una: una,** adv., together
     sepulta: sepelio, sepelire, sepelivi, sepultum, bury
     domus: domus, -us, f., house, home

23   Note the numerous references in lines 19–23 to Catullus' brother; these dramatically convey the pervasive depth of the poet's personal suffering at the loss of his beloved **frater.**

24   **alebat: alo, alere, alui, altum,** foster, support, nourish

25 **interitu: interitus, -us,** m., fall, overthrow, destruction, death (ablative of cause)
　　fugavi: fugo, fugare, fugavi, fugatum, cause to flee, drive off, put to flight

27 **quod:** "the fact that"
　　Veronae: Verona, -ae, f., the city of Verona where Catullus has a family home distinct
　　　　from his personal residence in Rome; the locative case here means "at Verona".
　　turpe: turpis, -e, adj., base, bad, shameful

28 **quod:** "because"
　　nota: nota, notae, f., stamp, type, quality

29 **tepefactet: tepefacto, tepefactare, tepefactavi, tepefactatum,** warm, make warm, be in
　　　　the habit of warming; "must make warm," but the text here is corrupt.
　　cubili: cubile, -is, n., resting place, bed

30 **id: id** sums up all that has gone before.

31 **ignosces: ignosco, ignoscere, ignovi, ignotum,** pardon
　　ademit: adimo, adimere, ademi, ademptum, remove, take away

32 **nequeo: nequeo, nequire, nequivi, nequitum,** be unable

33 **scriptorum: scriptum, -i,** n., writing, book

34 **hoc fit:** Catullus offers a reason for his lack of books in Verona.

35 **carpitur: carpo, carpere, carpsi, carptum,** pick, pluck, enjoy, snatch; here in the sense of
　　　　"is past" or "is spent"

36 **huc: huc** means "here in Verona".
　　capsula: capsula, -ae, f., small cylindrical box for carrying a scroll

37 **quod cum ita sit:** here in the sense of "since this is the way it is"
　　nolim is a volitive subjunctive that introduces a substantive clause (**statuas**) with **ut**
　　　　understood.
　　statuas: statuo, statuere, statui, statutum, determine, conclude, judge

38 **ingenuo: ingenuus-a-um,** adj., open, noble, generous

39 **utriusque: uterque-utraque-utrumque,** adj., each, both; referring perhaps to Manlius'
　　　　desire for both the poems authored by Catullus and the translations he has made of
　　　　earlier Greek poets
　　posta est=posita est: pono, ponere, posui, positum, make, serve, lay down

40 **ultro: ultro,** adv., willingly
　　deferrem: defero, deferre, detuli, delatum, offer, confer
　　siqua=si qua

69

According to this poem, which marks the beginning of the short elegiac poems that will make up the rest of the Catullan corpus, Rufus, probably Caelius Rufus, lover of Lesbia and client of the Roman orator Marcus Tullius Cicero, suffers from severe body odor. Catullus suggests that this problem is the reason why women wish to avoid him. The meter is elegiac distich.

> Noli admirari, quare tibi femina nulla,
>   Rufe, velit tenerum supposuisse femur,
> non si illam rarae labefactes munere vestis
>   aut perluciduli deliciis lapidis.
> laedit te quaedam mala fabula, qua tibi fertur   5
>   valle sub alarum trux habitare caper.
> hunc metuunt omnes, neque mirum: nam mala valde est
>   bestia, nec quicum bella puella cubet.
> quare aut crudelem nasorum interfice pestem,
>   aut admirari desine cur fugiunt.   10

1   **admirari: admiror, admirari, admiratus sum,** wonder, be surprised at

2   **supposuisse=supponere: suppono, supponere, supposui, suppositum,** put under
femur: femur, femoris, n., thigh

3   **rarae: rarus-a-um,** adj., scarce, rare, uncommon
labefactes: labefacto, labefactare, labefactavi, labefactatum, weaken

4   **perluciduli: perlucidulus-a-um,** adj., transparent
deliciis: deliciae, -arum, f., delight, charm; here in the sense of "luxuries"

5   **laedit: laedo, laedere, laesi, laesum,** hurt
fabula: fabula, -ae, f., story, rumor

6   **alarum: ala, alae,** f., wing, arm, arm-pit
trux: trux, trucis, adj., savage, wild
caper: caper, capri, m., goat

7   **valde: valde,** adv., very, intensely

8   **quicum=quacum,** referring to **bestia**
cubet: cubo, cubare, cubui, cubitum, recline, lie down; here "would recline"

9   **interfice: interficio, interficere, interfeci, interfectum,** kill, destroy

10   **fugiunt** is a present indicative active form instead of the present subjunctive active form which the indirect question would demand; this is done to add vividness to the poet's final comment.

116

This final poem in the corpus is addressed to Lucius Gellius Poplicola, a noted rival of Catullus for Lesbia's affections. Associated with Clodius, the brother of Lesbia (Clodia), once prosecuted by Cicero, Gellius appears in several of Catullus' earlier poems (74, 80, 88, 89, 90, and 91). He is presented as a very sordid character. Here Catullus references past attempts at reconciliation, but resolves in the end to remain effectively at war with him. The meter is elegiac distich.

> Saepe tibi studioso animo venante requirens
>   carmina uti possem mittere Battiadae,
> qui te lenirem nobis, neu conarere
>   tela infesta meum mittere in usque caput,
> hunc video mihi nunc frustra sumptum esse laborem,   5
>   Gelli, nec nostras hic valuisse preces.
> contra nos tela ista tua evitabimus acta:
>   at fixus nostris tu dabis supplicium.

1   **venante: venor, venari, venatus sum**, hunt
     requirens: requiro, requirere, requisivi, requisitum, search for, seek

2   **uti=ut**, conj., how
     Battiadae: see Poem 65 line 16; **carmina...Battiadae**=poems of Callimachus

3   **qui=quibus**, by which
     lenirem: lenio, lenire, lenivi, lenitum, appease, soothe; **lenirem** is subjunctive in a
          relative clause of purpose.
     nobis=mihi; here in the sense of "towards me"
     neu=neve, adv., nor, and not
     conarere=conareris: conor, conari, conatus sum, try, attempt; **conarere** is a syncopated
          imperfect subjunctive in a negative result clause; this line is entirely composed of
          spondees.

4   **tela: telum, -i**, n., shaft, barb, sword
     infesta: infestus-a-um, adj., unsafe, hostile; note how **mittere** contrasts with **mittere** in
          line 2.
     in usque caput: "all the way to my head"

5   **mihi**, dative of agent with **sumptum esse**; "was undertaken by me"

6   **nostras=meas**
     hic=in hac re, in this matter
     valuisse: valeo, valere, valui, valitum, prevail

7   **nos=me**
     evitabimus=evitabo
     acta: ago, agere, egi, actum, put forth; here "launched"

8   **fixus: figo, figere, fixi, fictum**, strike, pierce
     nostris, understand **telis; nostris=meis**, a reference to Catullus' earlier poems, particularly
          91, which attack Gellius
     dabis supplicium: in the sense of "pay the penalty"; the final "*i*" in **dabis** must be short
          to fit the meter.

Poems

Latin Text only

14a

Ni te plus oculis meis amarem,
iucundissime Calve, munere isto
odissem te odio Vatiniano:
nam quid feci ego quidve sum locutus,
cur me tot male perderes poetis?   5
isti di mala multa dent clienti,
qui tantum tibi misit impiorum.
quod si, ut suspicor, hoc novum ac repertum
munus dat tibi Sulla litterator,
non est mi male, sed bene ac beate,   10
quod non dispereunt tui labores.
di magni, horribilem et sacrum libellum,
quem tu scilicet ad tuum Catullum
misti, continuo ut die periret
Saturnalibus, optimo dierum!   15
non non hoc tibi, salse, sic abibit:
nam, si luxerit, ad librariorum
curram scrinia, Caesios, Aquinos,
Suffenum, omnia colligam venena,
ac te his suppliciis remunerabor.   20
vos hinc interea valete abite
illuc, unde malum pedem attulistis,
saecli incommoda, pessimi poetae.

30

Alfene immemor atque unanimis false sodalibus,
iam te nil miseret, dure, tui dulcis amiculi?
iam me prodere, iam non dubitas fallere, perfide?
nec facta impia fallacum hominum caelicolis placent.
quae tu neglegis, ac me miserum deseris in malis;   5
eheu quid faciant, dic, homines cuive habeant fidem?
certe tute iubebas animam tradere, inique, <me>
inducens in amorem, quasi tuta omnia mi forent.
idem nunc retrahis te ac tua dicta omnia factaque
ventos irrita ferre ac nebulas aereas sinis.   10
si tu oblitus es, at di meminerunt, meminit Fides,
quae te ut paeniteat postmodo facti faciet tui.

40

Quaenam te mala mens, miselle Ravide,
agit praecipitem in meos iambos?
quis deus tibi non bene advocatus
vecordem parat excitare rixam?
an ut pervenias in ora vulgi?   5
quid vis? qualubet esse notus optas?
eris, quandoquidem meos amores
cum longa voluisti amare poena.

60

Num te leaena montibus Libystinis
aut Scylla latrans infima inguinum parte
tam mente dura procreavit ac taetra,
ut supplicis vocem in novissimo casu
contemptam haberes, a nimis fero corde?   5

64

Haec vestis priscis hominum variata figuris   50
heroum mira virtutes indicat arte.
namque fluentisono prospectans litore Diae,
Thesea cedentem celeri cum classe tuetur
indomitos in corde gerens Ariadna furores,
necdum etiam sese quae visit visere credit,   55
utpote fallaci quae tum primum excita somno
desertam in sola miseram se cernat harena.
immemor at iuvenis fugiens pellit vada remis,
irrita ventosae linquens promissa procellae.
    Quem procul ex alga maestis Minois ocellis, 60
saxea ut effigies bacchantis prospicit, eheu,
prospicit et magnis curarum fluctuat undis,
non flavo retinens subtilem vertice mitram,
non contecta levi velatum pectus amictu,
non tereti strophio lactentis vincta papillas,   65
omnia quae toto delapsa e corpore passim
ipsius ante pedes fluctus salis adludebant.

sed neque tum mitrae neque tum fluitantis amictus
illa vicem curans toto ex te pectore, Theseu,
toto animo, tota pendebat perdita mente. 70
a misera, assiduis quam luctibus externavit
spinosas Erycina serens in pectore curas,
illa tempestate, ferox quo tempore Theseus
egressus curvis e litoribus Piraei
attigit iniusti regis Gortynia templa. 75
    Nam perhibent olim crudeli peste coactam
Androgeoneae poenas exsolvere caedis
electos iuvenes simul et decus innuptarum
Cecropiam solitam esse dapem dare Minotauro.
quis angusta malis cum moenia vexarentur, 80
ipse suum Theseus pro caris corpus Athenis
proicere optavit potius quam talia Cretam
funera Cecropiae nec funera portarentur.
atque ita nave levi nitens ac lenibus auris
magnanimum ad Minoa venit sedesque superbas. 85
hunc simul ac cupido conspexit lumine virgo
regia, quam suavis expirans castus odores
lectulus in molli complexu matris alebat,
quales Eurotae progignunt flumina myrtos
aurave distinctos educit verna colores, 90
non prius ex illo flagrantia declinavit
lumina, quam cuncto concepit corpore flammam
funditus atque imis exarsit tota medullis.
heu misere exagitans immiti corde furores
sancte puer, curis hominum qui gaudia misces, 95
quaeque regis Golgos quaeque Idalium frondosum,
qualibus incensam iactastis mente puellam
fluctibus in flavo saepe hospite suspirantem!
quantos illa tulit languenti corde timores!
quanto saepe magis fulgore expalluit auri, 100
cum saevum cupiens contra contendere monstrum
aut mortem appeteret Theseus aut praemia laudis!
non ingrata tamen frustra munuscula divis
promittens tacito suscepit vota labello.
nam velut in summo quatientem bracchia Tauro 105
quercum aut conigeram sudanti cortice pinum
indomitus turbo contorquens flamine robur,
eruit (illa procul radicitus exturbata
prona cadit, late quaevis cumque obvia frangens),
sic domito saevum prostravit corpore Theseus 110
nequiquam vanis iactantem cornua ventis.

inde pedem sospes multa cum laude reflexit
errabunda regens tenui vestigia filo,
ne labyrintheis e flexibus egredientem
tecti frustraretur inobservabilis error.   115
   Sed quid ego a primo digressus carmine plura
commemorem, ut linquens genitoris filia vultum,
ut consanguineae complexum, ut denique matris,
quae misera in gnata deperdita laeta<batur>,
omnibus his Thesei dulcem praeoptarit amorem: 120
aut ut vecta rati spumosa ad litora Diae,
<venerit> aut ut eam devinctam lumina somno
liquerit immemori discedens pectore coniunx?
saepe illam perhibent ardenti corde furentem
clarisonas imo fudisse e pectore voces,   125
ac tum praeruptos tristem conscendere montes,
unde aciem <in> pelagi vastos protenderet aestus,
tum tremuli salis adversas procurrere in undas
mollia nudatae tollentem tegmina surae,
atque haec extremis maestam dixisse querellis,   130
frigidulos udo singultus ore cientem:
   "Sicine me patriis avectam, perfide, ab aris,
perfide, deserto liquisti in litore, Theseu?
sicine discedens neglecto numine divum,
immemor a! devota domum periuria portas?   135
nullane res potuit crudelis flectere mentis
consilium? tibi nulla fuit clementia praesto,
immite ut nostri vellet miserescere pectus?
at non haec quondam blanda promissa dedisti
voce mihi; non haec miserae sperare iubebas,   140
sed conubia laeta, sed optatos hymenaeos,
quae cuncta aerii discerpunt irrita venti.
nunc iam nulla viro iuranti femina credat,
nulla viri speret sermones esse fideles;
quis dum aliquid cupiens animus praegestit apisci,   145
nil metuunt iurare, nihil promittere parcunt:
sed simul ac cupidae mentis satiata libido est,
dicta nihil metuere, nihil periuria curant.
certe ego te in medio versantem turbine leti
eripui, et potius germanum amittere crevi,   150
quam tibi fallaci supremo in tempore dessem.
pro quo dilaceranda feris dabor alitibusque
praeda, neque iniacta tumulabor mortua terra.
quaenam te genuit sola sub rupe leaena?
quod mare conceptum spumantibus exspuit undis,   155

quae Syrtis, quae Scylla rapax, quae vasta Carybdis,
talia qui reddis pro dulci praemia vita?
si tibi non cordi fuerant conubia nostra,
saeva quod horrebas prisci praecepta parentis,
attamen in vestras potuisti ducere sedes,   160
quae tibi iucundo famularer serva labore,
candida permulcens liquidis vestigia lymphis,
pupureave tuum consternens veste cubile.
   Sed quid ego ignaris nequiquam conquerar auris,
externata malo, quae nullis sensibus auctae   165
nec missas audire queunt nec reddere voces?
ille autem prope iam mediis versatur in undis,
nec quisquam apparet vacua mortalis in alga.
sic nimis insultans extremo tempore saeva
fors etiam nostris invidit questibus auris.   170
   Iuppiter omnipotens, utinam ne tempore primo
Cnosia Cecropiae tetigissent litora puppes,
indomito nec dira ferens stipendia tauro
perfidus in Creta religasset navita funem,
nec malus hic celans dulci crudelia forma   175
consilia in nostris requiesset sedibus hospes!
nam quo me referam? Quali spe perdita nitor?
Idaeosne petam montes? At gurgite lato
discernens ponti truculentum dividit aequor.
an patris auxilium sperem? Quemne ipsa reliqui,   180
respersum iuvenem fraterna caede secuta?
coniugis an fido consoler memet amore?
quine fugit lentos incurvans gurgite remos?
praeterea nullo colitur sola insula tecto,
nec patet egressus pelagi cingentibus undis.   185
nulla fugae ratio, nulla spes: omnia muta,
omnia sunt deserta, ostentant omnia letum.
non tamen ante mihi languescent lumina morte,
nec prius a fesso secedent corpore sensus,
quam iustam a divis exposcam prodita multam   190
caelestumque fidem postrema comprecer hora.
  "Quare facta virum multantes vindice poena,
Eumenides, quibus anguino redimita capillo
frons expirantis praeportat pectoris iras,
huc huc adventate, meas audite querellas,   195
quas ego, vae misera, extremis proferre medullis
cogor inops, ardens, amenti caeca furore.
quae quoniam verae nascuntur pectore ab imo,
vos nolite pati nostrum vanescere luctum,

sed quali solam Theseus me mente reliquit,　　　　　200
tali mente, deae, funestet seque suosque."
　Has postquam maesto profudit pectore voces,
supplicium saevis exposcens anxia factis,
annuit invicto caelestum numine rector;
quo motu tellus atque horrida contremuerunt　　　205
aequora concussitque micantia sidera mundus.
ipse autem caeca mentem caligine Theseus
consitus oblito dimisit pectore cuncta,
quae mandata prius constanti mente tenebat,
dulcia nec maesto sustollens signa parenti　　　　210
sospitem Erectheum se ostendit visere portum.
　Namque ferunt olim, classi cum moenia divae
linquentem gnatum ventis concrederet Aegeus,
talia complexum iuveni mandata dedisse:
　"Gnate mihi longa iucundior unice vita,　　　　215
gnate, ego quem in dubios cogor dimittere casus,
reddite in extrema nuper mihi fine senectae,
quandoquidem fortuna mea ac tua fervida virtus
eripit invito mihi te, cui languida nondum
lumina sunt gnati cara saturata figura,　　　　　220
non ego te gaudens laetanti pectore mittam,
nec te ferre sinam fortunae signa secundae,
sed primum multas expromam mente querellas,
canitiem terra atque infuso pulvere foedans,
inde infecta vago suspendam lintea malo,　　　　225
nostros ut luctus nostraeque incendia mentis
carbasus obscurata dicet ferrugine Hibera.
quod tibi si sancti concesserit incola Itoni,
quae nostrum genus ac sedes defendere Erecthei
annuit, ut tauri respergas sanguine dextram,　　230
tum vero facito ut memori tibi condita corde
haec vigeant mandata, nec ulla oblitteret aetas;
ut simul ac nostros invisent lumina collis,
funestam antennae deponant undique vestem,
candidaque intorti sustollant vela rudentes,　　235
quam primum cernens ut laeta gaudia mente
agnoscam, cum te reducem aetas prospera sistet."
　Haec mandata prius constanti mente tenentem
Thesea ceu pulsae ventorum flamine nubes
aereum nivei montis liquere cacumen.　　　　　240
at pater, ut summa prospectum ex arce petebat,
anxia in assiduos absumens lumina fletus,
cum primum infecti conspexit lintea veli,

praecipitem sese scopulorum e vertice iecit,
amissum credens immiti Thesea fato. 245
sic funesta domus ingressus tecta paterna
morte ferox Theseus, qualem Minoidi luctum
obtulerat mente immemori, talem ipse recepit.
quae tum prospectans cedentem maesta carinam
multiplices animo volvebat saucia curas. 250
  At parte ex alia florens volitabat Iacchus
cum thiaso Satyrorum et Nysigenis Silenis,
te quaerens, Ariadna, tuoque incensus amore.

65

Etsi me assiduo confectum cura dolore
    sevocat a doctis, Hortale, virginibus,
nec potis est dulcis Musarum expromere fetus
    mens animi (tantis fluctuat ipsa malis:
namque mei nuper Lethaeo gurgite fratris 5
    pallidulum manans alluit unda pedem,
Troia Rhoeteo quem subter litore tellus
    ereptum nostris obterit ex oculis—

----

    numquam ego te, vita frater amabilior, 10
aspiciam posthac? at certe semper amabo,
    semper maesta tua carmina morte canam,
qualia sub densis ramorum concinit umbris
    Daulias absumpti fata gemens Ityli):
sed tamen in tantis maeroribus, Hortale, mitto 15
    haec expressa tibi carmina Battiadae,
ne tua dicta vagis nequiquam credita ventis
    effluxisse meo forte putes animo,
ut missum sponsi furtivo munere malum
    procurrit casto virginis e gremio, 20
quod miserae oblitae molli sub veste locatum,
    dum adventu matris prosilit, excutitur;
atque illud prono praeceps agitur decursu,
    huic manat tristi conscius ore rubor.

68

quod mihi fortuna casuque oppressus acerbo
    conscriptum hoc lacrimis mittis epistolium,
naufragum ut eiectum spumantibus aequoris undis
    sublevem et a mortis limine restituam,
quem neque sancta Venus molli requiescere somno   5
    desertum in lecto caelibe perpetitur,
nec veterum dulci scriptorum carmine Musae
    oblectant, cum mens anxia pervigilat;
id gratum est mihi, me quoniam tibi dicis amicum,
    muneraque et Musarum hinc petis et Veneris;   10
sed tibi ne mea sint ignota incommoda, Manli
    neu me odisse putes hospitis officium,
accipe, quis merser fortunae fluctibus ipse,
    ne amplius a misero dona beata petas.
tempore quo primum vestis mihi tradita pura est,   15
    iucundum cum aetas florida ver ageret,
multa satis lusi: non est dea nescia nostri,
    quae dulcem curis miscet amaritiem;
sed totum hoc studium luctu fraterna mihi mors
    abstulit. o misero frater adempte mihi,   20
tu mea tu moriens fregisti commoda, frater,
    tecum una tota est nostra sepulta domus,
omnia tecum una perierunt gaudia nostra,
    quae tuus in vita dulcis alebat amor.
cuius ego interitu tota de mente fugavi   25
    haec studia atque omnes delicias animi.
quare, quod scribes Veronae turpe Catullo
    esse, quod hic quisquis de meliore nota
frigida deserto tepefactat membra cubili,
    id, Manli, non est turpe, magis miserum est.   30
ignosces igitur, si, quae mihi luctus ademit,
    haec tibi non tribuo munera, cum nequeo.
nam, quod scriptorum non magna est copia apud me,
    hoc fit, quod Romae vivimus: illa domus,
illa mihi sedes, illic mea carpitur aetas: 35
    huc una ex multis capsula me sequitur.
quod cum ita sit, nolim statuas nos mente maligna
    id facere aut animo non satis ingenuo,
quod tibi non utriusque petenti copia posta est:
    ultro ego deferrem, copia siqua foret.   40

69

Noli admirari, quare tibi femina nulla,
    Rufe, velit tenerum supposuisse femur,
non si illam rarae labefactes munere vestis
    aut perluciduli deliciis lapidis.
laedit te quaedam mala fabula, qua tibi fertur   5
    valle sub alarum trux habitare caper.
hunc metuunt omnes, neque mirum: nam mala valde est
    bestia, nec quicum bella puella cubet.
quare aut crudelem nasorum interfice pestem,
    aut admirari desine cur fugiunt.   10

116

Saepe tibi studioso animo venante requirens
    carmina uti possem mittere Battiadae,
qui te lenirem nobis, neu conarere
    tela infesta meum mittere in usque caput,
hunc video mihi nunc frustra sumptum esse laborem,   5
    Gelli, nec nostras hic valuisse preces.
contra nos tela ista tua evitabimus acta:
    at fixus nostris tu dabis supplicium.

Vocabulary

—A—

a, inter., ah! (an interjection expressing various feelings such as regret, distress, pity)

abeo, abire, abii, come out, come off, be allowed to pass

absumo, absumere, absumpsi, absumptum, exhaust, consume, kill

accipio, accipere, accepi, acceptum, receive, hear

acies, -ei, f., gaze, sight

adimo, adimere, ademi, ademptum, remove, take away

adludo, adludere, adlusi, adlusum, play, play with

adluo, adluere, adlui, flow near to, wash over

admiror, admirari, admiratus sum, wonder, be surprised at

adnuo, adnuere, adnui, adnutum, assent, promise

adsiduus-a-um, adj., incessant

advento, adventare, adventavi, adventatum, come in haste, advance

advoco, advocare, advocavi, advocatum, invoke

Aegeus, -i, m., Aegeus, father of Theseus, King of Athens

aereus-a-um, adj., copper or bronze colored

aerius-a-um, adj., lofty

aestus, -us, m., tide, surge of the sea

aetas, aetatis, f., life, time

agnosco, agnoscere, agnovi, agnitum, know once more

ago, agere, egi, actum, put forth, drive, do, pass

ala, alae, f., wing, arm, arm-pit

ales, alitis, f., bird

alga, -ae, f., sea-weed

alo, alere, alui, altum, rear, raise, foster, support, nourish

amarities, -ei, f., bitterness

amictus, -us, m., dress, clothing, garment

amplius, adv., any longer

Androgeoneus-a-um, adj., of or pertaining to Androgeus, a son of King Minos,

anguinus-a-um, adj., snaky

angustus-a-um narrow

antenna, -ae, f., the yardarm of a ship

anxius-a-um, adj., troubled

apiscor, apisci, aptus sum, obtain, get

Ariadna, -ae, f., daughter of Minos, King of Crete

assiduus-a-um, adj., continually present, constant

at, conj., yet

attamen, conj., even so, nevertheless

attingo, attingere, attigi, attactum, touch, arrive at

augeo, augere, auxi, auctum, increase, enlarge, bless (endow) with

aura, -ae, f., wind, breeze, air

auris, -is, f., ear

—B—

bacchor, bacchari, bacchatus sum, to rave like a Bacchant (a wild devotee of Bacchus)

blandus-a-um, adj., smooth, charming

—C—

cacumen, cacuminis, n., summit

caedes, caedis, f., murder

caelebs, caelibis, adj., unmarried, single

caligo, caliginis, f., mist, fog

canities, -ei, f., grey hair

caper, capri, m., goat

capillus, -i, m., hair

capsula, -ae, f., small cylindrical box for carrying a scroll

carbasus, -i, f., sail

carina, -ae, f., ship

carpo, carpere, carpsi, carptum, pick, pluck, enjoy, snatch

castus-a-um, adj., chaste, pure, innocent

casus, -us, m., event, misfortune, crisis

Cecropius-a-um, adj., Athenian, from King Cecrops of Athens

cerno, cernere, crevi, cretum, decide, see

ceu, adv., just as

Charybdis, -is, f., Charybdis, a monster in the Straits of Messina

cieo, ciere, civi, citum, call forth, invoke

cingo, cingere, cinxi, cinctum, surround, enclose

clarisonus-a-um, adj., clear sounding, loud and clear

cliens, clientis, m., client

colligo, colligere, collegi, collectum, gather, collect

collis, -is, m., hill

colo, colere, colui, cultum, inhabit

commemoro, commemorare, commemoravi, commemoratum, relate, recall

commodum, -i, n., advantage

complector, complecti, complexus sum, embrace, clasp

comprecor, comprecari, comprecatus sum, implore, supplicate

concedo, concedere, concessi, concessum, allow, grant

concino, concinere, concinui, sound, sing

concipio, concipere, concepi, conceptum, conceive

condo, condere, condidi, conditum, preserve, store, write

conficio, conficere, confeci, confectum, complete

coniger, conigera, conigerum, adj., cone-bearing

conor, conari, conatus sum, try, attempt

conqueror, conqueri, conquestus sum, complain, bewail

conscius-a-um, adj., knowing, guilty

conscribo, conscribere, conscripsi, conscriptum, write

consero, conserere, consevi, consitum, cover, plant, sow

consilium, consilii, n., decision, plan

consolor, consolari, consolatus sum, console, comfort, cheer

consterno, consternere, constravi, constratum, cover

contego, contegere, contexi, contectum, cover, hide, conceal

contemptus-a-um, adj., despised, despicable

continuus-a-um, adj., following

contorqueo, contorquere, contorsi, contortum, twist, turn

contremo, contremere, contremui, tremble, quake

cor, cordis, n., heart

cortex, corticis, m./f., bark

Creta, -ae, f., Crete

cubile, -is, n., bed, couch, resting place

cubo, cubare, cubui, cubitum, recline, lie down

cum primum, adv., as soon as

cur, conj., why

—D—

daps, dapis, f., religious feast, a sacrificial meal

Daulias, Dauliadis, adj., of or pertaining to Daulis

declino, declinare, declinavi, declinatum, turn aside, lower

decursus, -us, m., descent, fall

decus, decoris, n., glory

defero, deferre, detuli, delatum, offer, confer

deliciae, -arum, f., delight, charm

deperdo, deperdere, deperdidi, deperditum, ruin, destroy

desertus-a-um, adj., abandoned, left alone

desum, deesse, defui, fail (with the dative case)

devincio, devincire, devinxi, devinctum, bind

devotus-a-um, adj., accursed

Dia, -ae, f., Dia is the name of an island north of Crete

dilacero, dilacerare, dilaceravi, dilaceratum, tear to pieces

discerno, discernere, discrevi, discretum, separate

discerpo, discerpere, discerpsi, discerptum, disperse, tear apart

dispereo, disperire, disperii, to go to ruin, be undone, perish

domo, domare, domui, domitum, tame, conquer, break, subdue

domus, -us, f., house, home

—E—

effigies, -ei, f., statue, image

egredior, egredi, egressus sum, go out, put to sea

eheu, interj., alas

eicio, eicere, eieci, eiectum, run aground

eligo, eligere, elegi, electum, choose, pick

epistolium, epistolii, n., short letter

Erec(h)theus-a-um, adj., Athenian, from the name of Erechtheus, a legendary king of Athens

errabundus-a-um, adj., wandering

error, erroris, m., maze, wandering

eruo, eruere, erui, erutum, uproot

Erycinus-a-um, adj., of or pertaining to Mt. Eryx in Sicily, sacred to Venus, an epithet for Venus

Eumenides, Eumenidum, f., the Furies, the avenging goddesses with snakes in their hair

Eurotas, -ae, m., the Eurotas, a river in southern Greece

exagito, exagitare, exagitavi, exagitatum, incite, disturb, excite

exardesco, exardescere, exarsi, exarsum, blaze out, kindle, take fire

excutio, excutere, excussi, excussum, shake out

expallesco, expallescere, expallui, expallitum, turn pale

exprimo, exprimere, expressi, expressum, translate

expromo, expromere, exprompsi, expromptum, show forth, display, bring forth, state, disclose

exsolvo, exsolvere, exsolvi, exsolutum, pay, exact

exspiro, exspirare, exspiravi, exspiratum, breathe out, rush out

exspuo, exspuere, exspui, exsputum, spit out

externo, externare, externavi, externatum, terrify, make mad

exturbo, exturbare, exturbavi, exturbatum, force out, knock out

—F—

fabula, -ae, f., story, rumor

facio, facere, feci, factum, make, do

fallax, fallacis, adj., deceitful, deceptive

fallo, fallere, fefelli, falsum, deceive

falsus-a-um, adj., false, disloyal

famulor, famulari, famulatus sum, serve

femur, femoris, n., thigh

ferrugo, ferruginis, f., rust, dark color

ferus, -i, m., beast

ferus-a-um, adj., hard, fierce, wild

fervidus-a-um, adj., fiery

fetus, fetus, m., offspring

figo, figere, fixi, fictum, strike, pierce

filum, -i, n., thread, string

flagrans, flagrantis, adj., burning, glowing, blazing

flamen, flaminis, n., gale, wind

flavus-a-um, adj., golden, yellow, blonde

fletus, -us, m., weeping, tears

flexus, -us, m., winding

florens, florentis, adj., blooming, shining, bright, youthful

floridus-a-um, adj., blooming, beautiful

fluctuo, fluctuare, fluctuavi, fluctuatum, move in waves, waver, vacillate, toss

fluentisonus-a-um, adj., resounding with waves

fluito, fluitare, fluitavi, fluitatum, flow, float

foedo, foedare, foedavi, foedatum, befoul, mar, sully

fors, fortis, f., chance, luck

frango, frangere, fregi, fractum, break

frigidulus-a-um, adj., chilly

frondosus-a-um, adj., rich in leaves

frustror, frustrari, frustratus sum, trick, deceive

fugo, fugare, fugavi, fugatum, cause to flee, drive off, put to flight

fulgor, fulgoris, m., glitter, gleam, flash, brightness

funditus, adv., utterly, completely

fundo, fundere, fudi, fusum, pour, shed, utter

funesto, funestare, funestavi, funestatum, desecrate, stain with blood

funestus-a-um, adj., deadly, fatal, sorrowful

funis, -is, m., rope

funus, funeris, n., burial, corpse

furtivus-a-um, adj., stolen, secret

—G—

germanus, -i, m., brother

Gnosius-a-um, adj., of or belonging to Knossos, Cretan

Golgi, -orum, m., Golgi, a site on Cyprus, an island much associated with Venus

Gortynius-a-um, adj., Gortynian, from town of Gortyna on Crete

gremium, gremii, n., lap

—H—

heros, herois, m., hero

Hiberus-a-um, adj., Spanish

hinc, adv., from here

hospes, hospitis, m., guest, host

—I—

Iacchus, -i, m., Bacchus

iacto, iactare, iactavi, iactatum, throw, toss

iam, adv., now

iambus, -i, m., iambic poetry

Idaeus-a-um, adj., pertaining to the Ida mountain range on Crete

Idalium, Idalii, n., Idalium, a town on Cyprus also associated with Venus ignosco, ignoscere, ignovi, ignotum, pardon

immemor, immemoris, adj., unmindful (with the dative)

immitis, -e, adj., inexorable, severe

impius-a-um, adj., unworthy, (as a substantive) wrongdoer

incommodum, incommodi, n., trouble, loss, misfortune

incommodus-a-um, adj., troublesome, (as a substantive) trouble, misfortune

incurvo, incurvare, incurvavi, incurvatum, bend

indomitus-a-um, adj., wild, untamed

infestus-a-um, adj., unsafe, hostile

inficio, inficere, infeci, infectum, dye, discolor

infimus-a-um, adj., lowest

infundo, infundere, infudi, infusum, pour on

ingenuus-a-um, adj., open, noble, generous

inguen, inguinis, n., groin

inicio, inicere, inieci, iniectum, throw on

iniquus-a-um, adj., unfair, unjust

inobservabilis, -e, adj., unnoticed, untraceable

inops, inopis, adj., without resources, helpless

insulto, insultare, insultavi, insultatum, exult

interficio, interficere, interfeci, interfectum, kill, destroy

interitus, -us, m., fall, overthrow, destruction, death

intortus-a-um, adj., twisted

invideo, invidere, invidi, invisum, begrudge

inviso, invisere, invisi, invisum, look upon, see

irritus-a-um, adj., invalid, worthless, unsettled, null and void

Itonus, Itoni, f., Itonus, a town in Greece sacred to Athena, goddess of Athens

iubeo, iubere, iussi, iussum, order, compel

iuro, iurare, iuravi, iuratum, swear

—L—

labefacto, labefactare, labefactavi, labefactatum, weaken

labellum, -i, n., lip

labyrintheus-a-um, adj., labyrinthine, twisted, contorted

lactens, -entis, adj., milky, milk-white

laedo, laedere, laesi, laesum, hurt

laetor, laetari, laetatus sum, rejoice, take delight

lamentor, lamentari, lamentatus sum, weep, lament, bewail

languens, -entis, adj., faint, weak

languesco, languescere, langui, weaken, grow faint

languidus-a-um, adj., feeble, faint

latro, latrare, latravi, latratum, bark

leaena, -ae, f., lioness

lenio, lenire, lenivi, lenitum, appease, soothe

lentus-a-um, adj., tough, pliable

libido, libidinis, f., desire, passion

librarius-a-um, adj., pertaining to books, (as a substantive) transcriber of books

Libystinus-a-um, adj., African

linquo, linquere, liqui, leave, quit

linteum, -i, n., sail

liquidus- a-um, adj., pure, clean

loquor, loqui, locutus sum, speak, say

luceo, lucere, luxi, be light, be clear, shine

luctus, -us, m., mourning, lamentation

ludo, ludere, lusi, lusum, play, play at, sport with

lumen, luminis, n., light

lympha, -ae, f., water

—M—

maeror, maeroris, m., sadness, mourning

male, adv., badly

malum, -i, n., apple

malum, -i, n., evil, woe, misfortune

malus, -i, m., mast

mandatum, -i, n., command

mano, manare, manavi, manatum, flow, spread

medulla, -ae, f., marrow, bone marrow

memini, meminisse, remember

merso, mersare, mersavi, mersatum, dip, immerse, overwhelm

metuo, metuere, metui, metutum, fear

Minois, Minoidis, f., daughter of Minos (Ariadne)

misellus-a-um, adj., wretched, miserable, pathetic

misere, adv., wretchedly

misereo, miserere, miserui, take pity on, move someone to have pity for or on

miseresco, miserescere, feel pity for (with the genitive)

mitra, -ae, f., head-dress, bonnet, ceremonial cap or diadem

mitto, mittere, misi, missum, send

mollis, -e, adj., fine, soft, gentle

multa, -ae, f., penalty

multiplex, multiplicis, adj., manifold, various

multo, multare, multavi, multatum, punish

munus, muneris, n., gift

munusculum, -i, n., small present

myrtus, -i, f., myrtle

—N—

nata, -ae, f., daughter

natus-a-um, adj., born

natus, -i, m., son

naufragus, -i, m., a shipwrecked man

nauta, -ae, m., sailor

nebula, -ae, f., cloud

nequeo, nequire, nequivi, nequitum, be unable

neu or **neve,** adv., nor, and not

nimis, adv., too much, excessively

nitor, niti, nisus sum, depend on, press onward

niveus-a-um, adj., snowy

nota, notae, f., stamp, type, quality

novissimus-a-um, adj., newest, last, most recent

nuper, adv., recently

Nysigena, -ae, m., born on Mount Nysa (birthplace of Bacchus)

—O—

oblecto, oblectare, oblectavi, oblectatum, delight, please

oblittero, oblitterare, oblitteravi, oblitteratum, erase

oblitus-a-um, adj., forgetful

obliviscor, oblivisci, oblitus sum, forget

obscuro, obscurare, obscuravi, obscuratum, darken

obtero, obterere, obtrivi, obtritum, crush, trample

obvius-a-um, adj., in the way, so as to meet, meeting

odium, odii, n., hatred

officium, officii, n., duty, obligation

opprimo, opprimere, oppressi, oppressum, crush

os, oris, n., mouth, lips

ostento, ostentare, ostentavi, ostentatum, present to view, show, exhibit, hold out

—P—

paenitet, paenitere, paenituit, (impersonal verb) it pains

pallidulus-a-um, adj., rather dim, pale

papilla, -ae, f., breast

parco, parcere, peperci, parsum, refrain from, spare

pateo, patere, patui, be open, lie open, stand open

paternus-a-um, adj., paternal

patior, pati, passus sum, allow, permit

pello, pellere, pepuli, pulsum, beat, strike, push

perditus-a-um, adj., lost, desperate, hopeless, abandoned

perdo, perdere, perdidi, perditum, lose utterly, destroy

perhibeo, perhibere, perhibui, perhibitum, assert, call, say

periurium, periurii, n., perjury, lie

perlucidulus-a-um, adj., transparent

permulceo, permulcere, permulsi, permulsum, rub, soothe

perpetior, perpeti, perpessus sum, endure, permit, allow

pervenio, pervenire, perveni, perventum, reach, come to

pervigilo, pervigilare, pervigilavi, pervigilatum, stay awake all night

pes, pedis, m., foot

pinus, -i, f., pine

Piraeus, -i, m., Piraeus, the port of Athens

pono, ponere, posui, positum, make, serve, lay down

posthac, adv., in the future, hereafter

potius, adv., rather, more

praeceps, praecipitis, adj., head first

praeceptum, -i, n., order, command

praegestio, praegestire, be very eager, desire

praeopto, praeoptare, praeoptavi, praeoptatum, prefer

praeporto, praeportare, praeportavi, praeportatum, manifest, carry before

praeruptus-a-um, adj., sheer, steep

praesto, adv., at hand, ready

priscus-a-um, adj., ancient, venerable

prodo, prodere, prodidi, proditum, give up, surrender, abandon, betray

progigno, progignere, progenui, progenitum, beget, produce

pronus-a-um, adj., leaning forward, headlong, downwards

prope, adv., near

prosilio, prosilire, prosilui, jump up

prospecto, prospectare, prospectavi, prospectatum, look out, view

prospectus, -us, m., sight, view

prosperus-a-um, adj., fortunate, favorable, successful

purus-a-um, adj., pure, white

—Q—

qualis, -e, adj., just as, just like

qualubet or **qualibet,** adv., everywhere, where you will, in any way you please

quam primum, adv., as soon as possible

quandoquidem, conj., since indeed, seeing that, since

quatio, quatere, quassi, quassum, shake

queo, quire, quivi, quitum, be able, can

quercus, -us, f., oak

querella, -ae, f., lamentation, complaint

questus, -us, m., complaint, lament

quinam-quaenam-quodnam, inter. adj., what (a strong interrogative)

quiviscumque, quaeviscumque, quodviscumque, adj., any whatsoever

quoniam, conj., since now, whereas

—R—

radicitus, adv., by the roots, utterly

rarus-a-um, adj., scarce, rare, uncommon

ratis, -is, f., boat

rector, rectoris, m., master, here Zeus/Jupiter

redimio, redimire, redimii, redimitum, crown, encircle

redux, reducis, adj., brought back, returned

reflecto, reflectere, reflexi, reflexum, turn back, turn about

rego, regere, rexi, rectum, direct, guide, steer

religo, religare, religavi, religatum, moor, tie up

remuneror, remunerari, remuneratus sum, repay, reward

reperio, reperire, repperi, repertum, discover, devise

requiesco, requiescere, requievi, requietum, take rest, rest, find rest

requiro, requirere, requisivi, requisitum, search for, seek

respergo, respergere, respersi, respersum, sprinkle, stain

retraho, retrahere, retraxi, retractum, draw back

Rhoeteus-a-um, adj., of the promontory of Rhoeteum, near Troy

rixa, rixae, f., brawl, quarrel

robur, roboris, n., oak, here in the sense of tree trunk

rubor, ruboris, n., blush

rudens, rudentis, m., rope, (in the plural) rigging

—S—

sacer, sacra, sacrum, adj., sacred, holy

saeculum, -i, n., age, era

salsus-a-um, adj., witty, sharp, acute

satio, satiare, satiavi, satiatum, satisfy, fill

satis, adv., enough

Saturnalia, Saturnaliorum, n., festival of the Saturnalia

saturo, saturare, saturavi, saturatum, fill, satisfy

Satyrus, -i, m., a Satyr, a forest god associated with Bacchus and having goat's feet

saxeus-a-um, adj., rocky

scilicet, adv., for sure, of course

scrinium, scrinii, n., a cylindrical box or case for letters or scrolls

scriptum, -i, n., writing, book

Scylla, -ae, f., Scylla, a monster found in the Straits of Messina

secedo, secedere, secessi, secessum, withdraw, retire

secundus-a-um, adj., favorable, good

senecta, -ae, f., old age

sepelio, sepelire, sepelivi, sepultum, bury

sero, serere, sevi, satum, sow

sevoco, sevocare, sevocavi, sevocatum, separate, call away

sicine, adv., thus?, so?

Silenus, -i, m., a Silenus, one of a class of wood-spirits associated with Bacchus

simul ac, conj., as soon as

singultus, -us, m., sob, gasp

sino, sinere, sivi, situm, let, permit, allow

sisto, sistere, stiti, statum, present, produce

sodalis, -is, m., friend, comrade

solus-a-um, adj., only, alone, forsaken

sospes, sospitis, adj., safe, unhurt

spinosos-a-um, adj., thorny, difficult

sponsus, -i, m., bridegroom, lover

statuo, statuere, statui, statutum, determine, conclude, judge

stipendium, stipendii, n., tribute

strophium, strophii, n., breast-band

suavis, -e, adj., sweet, delightful

sublevo, sublevare, sublevavi, sublevatum, lift up

subter, prep. (with the ablative), below, underneath, close to

subtilis, -e, adj., finely woven, dainty, delicate

sudo, sudare, sudavi, sudatum, sweat, perspire

Suffenus, -i, m., Suffenus, a poet disliked by Catullus

supplex, supplicis, adj., (substantive) a supplicant

supplicium, supplicii, n., a bowing down, petition, punishment

suppono, supponere, supposui, suppositum, put under

sura, -ae, f., calf (of the leg)

suscipio, suscipere, suscepi, susceptum, take up, undertake, pledge

suspendo, suspendere, suspendi, suspensum, hang

suspicor, suspicari, suspicatus sum, suspect, suppose, conjecture

suspiro, suspirare, suspiravi, suspiratum, take a deep breath, heave a sigh

sustollo, sustollere, raise, lift up

Syrtis, -is, f., the Syrtis, a sand bank located on the Gulf of Sidra in North Africa

—T—

taeter-taetra-taetrum, adj., repulsive, offensive

tango, tangere, tetigi, tactum, touch, reach

tantus-a-um, adj., so much, so great

taurus, -i, m., bull

Taurus, Tauri, m., Taurus, a mountain range in southern Asia Minor

tegmen, tegminis, n., covering

telum, -i, n., shaft, barb, sword

tempestas, tempestatis, f., time, the weather, storm

tepefacto, tepefactare, tepefactavi, tepefactatum, warm, make warm, be in the habit of warming

teres, teretis, adj., elegant, shapely

thiasus, -i, m., a band of dancers

trado, tradere, tradidi, traditum, hand over, entrust

tremulus-a-um, adj., rippling, trembling

tristis, -e, adj., sad, mournful

truculentus-a-um, adj., wild, grim

trux, trucis, adj., savage, wild

tueor, tueri, tuitus sum, watch, see, look at

tumulo, tumulare, tumulavi, tumulatum, bury

turbo, turbinis, m., a whirlwind, tornado

turpis, -e, adj., base, bad, shameful

tute is the intensive form of **tu.**

—U—

udus-a-um, adj., wet

ultro, adv., willingly

una, adv., together

unanimus-a-um, adj., of one mind, faithful

unicus-a-um, adj., one and only

ut, conj., as (followed by the indicative mood)

uterque-utraque-utrumque, adj., each, both

utpote, adv., as is possible, seeing that, in as much as

—V—

vadum, -i, n., sea, water, shoal

vagus-a-um, adj., wandering, rambling, fickle

valde, adv., very, intensely

vanesco, vanescere, vanescui, come to nothing, disappear, pass away

vario, variare, variavi, variatum, vary

Vatinianus-a-um, adj., pertaining to Publius Vatinius

vecors, vecordis, adj., senseless, mad, insane

velo, velare, velavi, velatum, clothe, veil, conceal

velum, -i, n., sail

velut, adv., just as

venenum, -i, n., poison

venor, venari, venatus sum, hunt

ventosus-a-um, adj., windy, fickle, inconstant

ver, veris, n., spring

vernus-a-um, adj., of spring

Verona, -ae, f., the city of Verona

verso, versare, versavi, versatum, turn

vestigium, vestigii, n., footstep

vexo, vexare, vexavi, vexatum, trouble, harass, toss violently

vicem, accusative form of a defective noun for "change," used adverbially it means "for"

vigeo, vigere, vigui, thrive, live on

vincio, vincire, vinxi, vinctum, bind

vindex, vindicis, m./f., protector, deliveror, avenger

volito, volitare, volitavi, volitatum, fly about, flutter, move quickly

vulgus, -i, n., crowd, people